I took a horseback ride…I had a chance of seeing a little of this prairie country… This is said to be one of the richest portions of Mississippi…the scenery has little charm for me, although I could not but look with pleasure on the fine wheat and corn fields which are here in abundance. The enemy say they will starve us into submission. I do not think we run much risk of starving with fields such as these.[1]
—Kate Cummings, Confederate nurse, Okolona, Mississippi, June 1862

Major General Nathan Bedford Forrest (1821–1877).
"I think they are badly scared." February 21, 1864.
George and Katherine Davis Collection, Louisiana Research
Collection, Tulane University Libraries.

THE BATTLE OF
OKOLONA

DEFENDING THE MISSISSIPPI PRAIRIE

To Dearn, A
Daughter of Okolona
Brandon H. Beck
I hope you
enjoy this book.
Okolona is a
wonderful place.

BRANDON H. BECK
SERIES EDITOR DOUGLAS W. BOSTICK

Charleston | London

THE
History
PRESS

On the left is a dark blue wool mounted services jacket (1851) with yellow trim. A
"bummer" cap rests on a pair of sky blue kersey double seat trousers. The rifle is a Sharps
.59-caliber from 1859. On the right is a typical Confederate slouch hat. The jacket is
wool/cotton jean cloth, typical of those worn by Confederate cavalrymen. The saddle is
a U.S. McClellan saddle (1859), which was widely used by both Union and Confederate
cavalrymen. The trousers and kepi are typical Confederate gear, as are the knee boots. The
saber is an original piece, from 1860. *The objects shown in the photograph are from the collection of
Andy Anderson; photograph by Bob Price.*

Opposite: Resting on the McClellan saddle is a U.S. Army Colt revolver, .49-caliber. *The
objects shown in the photograph are from the collection of Andy Anderson; photograph by Bob Price.*

Published by The History Press
Charleston, SC 29403
www.historypress.net

Front cover image: *Southern Steel*, by Don Troiani. *Courtesy of the Military and Historical Image Bank. Back cover image*: Colonel Benjamin Grierson (right). Grierson was a successful and experienced cavalry raider, but he accompanied Smith's force without a formal command. *Photograph taken from* The Photographic History of the Civil War in Ten Volumes, *ed. Francis Trevelyan Miller, vol. 4.*

First published 2009

Manufactured in the United States

ISBN 978.1.59629.778.4

Library of Congress Cataloging-in-Publication Data

Beck, Brandon H., 1944-
The battle of Okolona : defending the Mississippi prairie / Brandon H. Beck.
p. cm.
Includes bibliographical references.
ISBN 978-1-59629-778-4
1. Okolona, Battle of, Miss., 1864. I. Title.
E476.14.B44 2009
976.2'05--dc22
2009042507

CONTENTS

ACKNOWLEDGEMENTS

I've been very fortunate in the help I've received in writing this book. The Mississippi Department of Archives and History (MDAH) is the indispensable starting point and sustaining force for historical research and writing in Mississippi. Jim Woodrick, in the Jackson office, and Jack Elliott, in Starkville, are skilled, knowledgeable and, above all, generous. They gave freely of their time and research. Thanks to them and their colleagues, MDAH preserves and enriches Mississippi's history.

Thanks to the Friends of the Battle of Okolona, Inc., much of the battlefield had been preserved, and an archive had been compiled before I began work. The organization's founder, Patsy Gregory, familiarized me with the sites, the archive and the town of Okolona. Andy Anderson, of Okolona, was also my guide and a source of information unobtainable anywhere else. It is his "living history" cavalry equipment that is pictured in this book. Gary Carnathan, of Okolona, owner of Beauwood, told me about its many associations with General Nathan Bedford Forrest. Sherman Carruthers, former mayor of Okolona, was the first person I met when I drove into town for the first time. He has long supported historic preservation and education. He is a good friend of Okolona's history and believes in Okolona's future. R.W. Chandler, also of Okolona, is steeped in local history. He is an accomplished writer and has committed much of his knowledge of Okolona to paper. In Columbus, at the Mississippi University for Women's J.C. Fant Memorial Library, Gail Gunter was indispensable in procuring the resources that I requested. General Parker Hills, of Clinton, Mississippi, shared his great knowledge with me, particularly in fixing the present-day locations of events that occurred 145 years ago. Bryan Horton, who had previously helped MDAH in its research, graciously allowed me access to his property, the site of Ivy's Hill. Estelle Ivy, librarian of the Okolona Carnegie Library, introduced me to the library's collection of sources in Okolona history, both literary and photographic. She found new sources as well. In West Point, I'm indebted to John McBryde, the authority on the Battle of Ellis Bridge. In Columbus, David Owen was a source of steady encouragement and my guide to Friendship Cemetery in Columbus. Bob Price, of Marietta, Georgia, took most of the present-day photographs in the book. He is a historian as well as a photographer, and he always goes the extra mile for another good picture. In Caledonia, Mississippi, Jessie Riggs helped throughout; at the end, he told me about Wayne Bradshaw's recent publication, *The Civil War Diary of William R. Dyer*, a member of Forrest's Escort. Elisa Shizak, president of the Columbus chapter of the United Daughters of the Confederacy, took the photographs of the paintings of Lee and Forrest at the Lee home in Columbus. She is a true historian. Reggie Swann, of Columbus, opened his library to me and shared his knowledge of the Prairie's historical landscape. The Columbus-Lowndes Public Library's local history room has a fine collection of historical sources and a wonderful atmosphere for research and writing. I always looked forward to my time there.

I would like to single out three authors whose books represent very early and very recent scholarship in Mississippi Civil War history: the late Margie Bearss (*Sherman's Forgotten Campaign* [1987]); Buck Foster (*Sherman's Mississippi Campaign* [2006]); and Ben Wynne (*Mississippi's Civil War: A Narrative History* [2006]).

My wife, Melissa, took several of the photographs and spent long hours preparing the manuscript for The History Press. She edited the text and also improved its style and content. I will always be grateful.

INTRODUCTION

The climactic year of the American Civil War was 1864, a year of unrelenting and ferocious combat. The year's first campaign was in Mississippi. In addition to heavy sustained fighting, 1864 brought with it widespread destruction of public and private property, designed to cripple the South's ability and will to continue the struggle. This, too, began in Mississippi.

In the interval between the fall of Vicksburg on July 4, 1863, and the beginning of the Atlanta Campaign in May 1864, General William T. Sherman planned to bring the war into the heart of Mississippi. He would lead an infantry force east from Vicksburg and Jackson to Meridian, where he was to be joined by General William Sooy Smith's cavalry force, coming southeast from Memphis and then down the line of the Mobile & Ohio Railroad from Okolona to Meridian. Sherman's force would number over twenty thousand men; Smith's force of over seven thousand was the largest raiding force yet assembled in the war in the west.

Smith's targets were the fields and storehouses of the rich Mississippi Prairie and the railroad that linked this "breadbasket" with the railroad junction at Meridian and the port of Mobile. It was the first significant campaign of 1864, a harbinger of the terrible conflict yet to come.

This book is a narrative of the campaign in the Mississippi Prairie in February 1864. It begins with a look at the Prairie and its railroad, the Mobile & Ohio. The second chapter covers the Union plans for the campaign and General William S. Smith. In the third chapter, the book turns to the

Confederate defense of the Prairie and to General Nathan Bedford Forrest. The next two chapters narrate the campaign itself, from Smith's arrival in the Prairie to Forrest's victory at Okolona. The battle's aftermath is the subject of the last chapter.

My prior work in Civil War history has been with the Army of Northern Virginia, particularly in another important Confederate "breadbasket," the Shenandoah Valley. The Mississippi Prairie and the Shenandoah Valley of Virginia are somewhat analogous, but there are crucial differences. In the Shenandoah Valley, Confederate forces were easily reinforced in time of need, along interior lines, from the main Confederate army east of the Blue Ridge. In Mississippi, however, the geographical and strategic situation was much different. In 1864, all that stood between the enemy and the Prairie was Forrest's small force. Today, just as Stonewall Jackson's name will always be linked with the Shenandoah Valley, Nathan Bedford Forrest's name will always be linked with the Prairie.

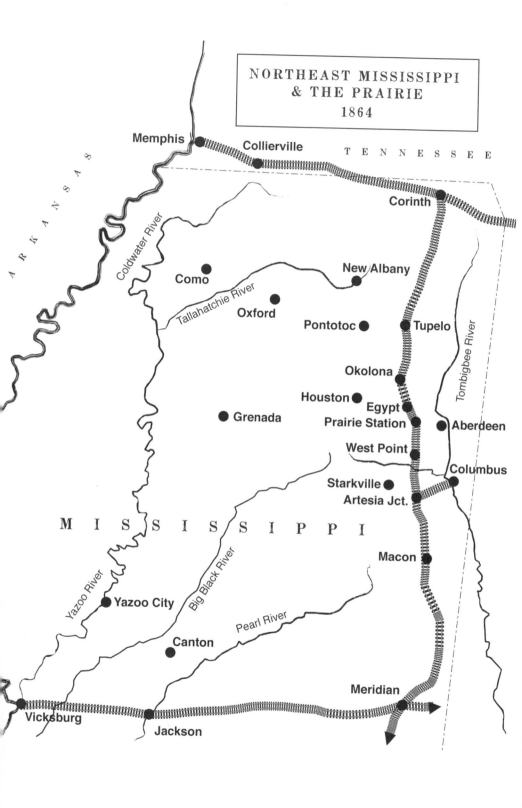

NORTHEAST MISSISSIPPI
& THE PRAIRIE
1864

Chapter 1

THE PRAIRIE AND THE RAILROAD

A cavalryman thinks first about his horse," wrote Confederate cavalryman James Dinkins. Horses fared well, he said, in the Prairie land of East Mississippi: "We found worlds of corn along the line of the Mobile & Ohio Railroad…the horses were fed all they could eat. It was a blessing to them."[2]

Lyman B. Pierce, sergeant and color bearer of the 2nd Iowa Cavalry, went further. He described the Prairie as "the breadbasket of the Confederacy."[3] Confederate president Jefferson Davis knew full well how important the Prairie had become by 1864, as Confederate military fortunes dimmed. In February 1864, Davis wrote to General Joseph E. Johnston, in command of the Army of Tennessee at Dalton, Georgia: "If deprived of the supplies in the interior of Mississippi and the Tombigbee Valley, the most disastrous consequences must ensue."[4]

The Mississippi Prairie lies west of the Tombigbee River, between it and the long Pontotoc Ridge. Known in geological terms as the North East Lime Region, its lime outcroppings have discouraged forestation and created "a strip of dark, clay-rich land running north and south…covered with scattered savannas of prairie."[5] It had long been a Chickasaw hunting ground. After the Chickasaw cession of 1832, however, settlers flooded the Prairie, giving rise to the "booming agricultural economy of the Tombigbee," complete with great plantations of cotton and corn.[6] The Tombigbee and its tributaries drain the land and provided Prairie planters with a connection to the port of Mobile. They sent their crops overland to Cotton Gin Port, the head of navigation for shipment to Mobile.[7] This changed with the coming of the Mobile & Ohio Railroad. The railroad transformed the Prairie almost as significantly as the coming of the first settlers.

The impetus for the railroad came from Mobile. The road's backers hoped to connect the great port on the Gulf with the Mississippi and Ohio Rivers through Alabama, Mississippi, Tennessee and Kentucky. The first state charters came in 1848. Surveyors and commissioners soon came north to determine the best route and to offer stock shares in towns along the proposed line.

There were few sales until track-laying gangs began working toward one another from Columbus, Kentucky, and Mobile. By May 1856, the northbound track was at Scooba Station, 178 miles from Mobile. But the railroad transformed the Prairie economy even before it was completed. Land under the plow and land values rose sharply. In 1850, the population of Chickasaw County was nearly 10,000, with 6,480 slaves. In 1860, there were 910 farms, 702 owned by slaveholders. Cotton production rose from 8,461 bales a year in 1840 to 26,494 by 1860. In 1857, the line carried 90,000 cotton bales to port. Corn increased similarly, to 862,256 bushels by 1860. Planters found that corn replenished soil exhausted by cotton; the usual pattern was to grow one acre of corn for every two acres of cotton. The number of hogs also grew, from 8,000 in 1840 to over 41,000 in 1850.[8]

Older towns not on the line, like Cotton Gin Port and Prairie Mount, declined, while railroad towns—West Point, Columbus, Okolona, Tupelo—rose and prospered.[9] West Point was a boomtown by 1859.[10] Okolona perhaps surpassed it, offering by 1859 a hospital and a women's college (Rose Gates). There were, in addition, dry goods stores, lawyers' and doctors' offices, blacksmiths, grocers, livery stables and tack stores.[11]

Workmen drove the railroad's ceremonial silver spike at Corinth on April 22, 1861. The completed line boasted 469 miles of five-foot gauge track. It was the longest (with some short gaps still) railroad under single ownership on the continent. There were sixty-eight engines on the locomotive roster. The company owned eight hundred freight cars and served eighty stations with passenger service. The Mobile–Meridian train made its scheduled run of 134 miles in seven hours. Proudly, the company pledged itself to the "support of southern commerce and the maintenance of southern institutions."[12] But these were already in the crucible of war. Mississippi left the Union on January 8, 1861, four months before the railroad's ceremony at Corinth. Nine days before the ceremony came news of Sumter.

The Prairie and the Railroad

With the coming of war, the region's importance as a breadbasket became clear. In January 1863, the president of the Mobile & Ohio Railroad, Milton Brown, noted that "the people of Mobile and the country above as far as Meridian are dependent on the prairie land for their supply of corn."[13] The war meant danger and hardship for the railroad and the Prairie. Both were strategically important, and both looked vulnerable. At Corinth, the Mobile & Ohio tracks crossed those of the Memphis & Charleston Railroad, known as "the vertebrae of the Confederacy." That crossing is still in heavy use. Corinth figured significantly in the Battle of Shiloh in April 1862. It then underwent a siege and Federal occupation. The loss of Corinth deprived the South of the use of the Memphis & Charleston, the most direct line of communication between the Confederate east and west. The Mobile & Ohio, however, remained in Confederate hands from Tupelo south. It was from Tupelo that General Braxton Bragg, commanding the Army of Tennessee, carried out the great troop transfer of July 1862, prior to his invasion of Kentucky. He brought the largest part of his army south on the Mobile & Ohio from Tupelo, through Meridian, to Mobile, and then north on other lines, finally to Chattanooga. The Mobile & Ohio was a target of General Ulysses S. Grant's cavalry during the Vicksburg Campaign in 1863. His final, successful effort to take Vicksburg included the spectacularly successful raid of Colonel Benjamin Grierson, April 17–May 2. Grierson's raid gave the eastern Prairie a brief foretaste of what was to come. His six-hundred-mile ride of devastation and mayhem drew Confederate attention away from Grant's crossing of the Mississippi River below Vicksburg. Confederate cavalry had been unable to concentrate against him. (General Nathan Bedford Forrest was, at that time, pursuing Colonel Abel Streight's raiders, whom he finally ran to ground near Rome, Georgia.) Although Grierson's men did some damage along the line of the Mobile & Ohio Railroad, the Prairie escaped the worst.

The fall of Vicksburg in July 1863 magnified Meridian's importance. It was the junction between the Mobile & Ohio and the Southern Railway of Mississippi.[14] Between the fall of Vicksburg and the beginning of the Atlanta Campaign in May 1864, Meridian became General William T. Sherman's strategic objective.

Columbus, on the Tombigbee, was linked by a short branch line to the main line at Artesia Springs, just to the west. The combination of railroad and riverboat service made Columbus an ideal manufacturing site. There were important works there, including an arsenal, cotton mill and shoe factory.[15]

Grierson's Cavalry, 1863. A portion of Colonel Benjamin Grierson's command in Baton Rouge, Louisiana, following Grierson's successful raid in Mississippi, April 17–May 2, 1863. *Photograph taken from* The Photographic History of the Civil War in Ten Volumes, *ed. Francis Trevelyan Miller, vol. 4.*

Okolona (previously Rose Hill) was incorporated in 1845. A postmaster, it is said, renamed it for a legendary Chickasaw chief. It was an important road junction as well as railroad town. Union Sergeant James Larson was there in 1864. He described the town as a "small but nicely built railroad town located on high ground and most of the houses were two storey buildings."[16] Many houses and at least one church became army hospitals. There were many of these in towns along the Mobile & Ohio, where nurses like Kate Cummings did their best for the carloads of wounded soldiers coming down from Shiloh and Corinth. Kate Cummings's hospital in Okolona was the largest of these.

The Prairie and the Railroad

The town had an additional distinction, pleasing to the eye and plain to see. It was the northern gateway to the Prairie. In 1864, Colonel George Waring, commanding a brigade in the Union force intent on devastating the Prairie, described the country north of Okolona as "rough, hopeless, God-forsaken...poor." But from Okolona southward, the Union cavalry saw spread out before it "a land flowing with milk and honey...known as the granary of the southern army...the evidence of wealth and fertility lay before us in all directions."[17] Sergeant Pierce marveled at "millions of bushels of corn, thousands of bales of cotton and the well filled smoke houses...countless wealth."[18]

The Prairie had not yet seen "Grim Visaged War."[19] That changed in 1864.

Chapter 2

"THEY HAVE INFORMATION OF OUR INTENTIONS"

Heaven intended on [Sherman] *to manifest depths of depravity yet untouched by a fallen race...unsated still in his demoniac vengeance to sweep over the country.*
—Macon Telegraph, *Macon, Georgia, December 5, 1864*[20]

Three disasters befell the Confederacy in the summer of 1863: the defeat at Gettysburg, July 1–3; the surrender of Vicksburg, July 4; and the fall of Chattanooga, September 8. The defeat at Gettysburg was a severe blow to the most powerful Confederate field army. The loss of Chattanooga stripped the South of an important railroad junction and endangered Atlanta, ninety miles south. The fall of Vicksburg was a great symbolic and material defeat. The fall of the Confederate "Gibraltar" freed the Mississippi River, as Lincoln said, to "flow unvexed to the sea." Losing the city also meant losing its garrison of over thirty thousand men. Losing the line of the river severed the Trans-Mississippi South from the Confederate states east of the river and opened the entire state of Mississippi to invasion and ruin.

These facts were immediately apparent to General Sherman, now heading the Military Division of the Mississippi. After Vicksburg, Sherman remained aggressive and restless. There were no large Confederate forces within easy reach, and the minor harassing activities of small guerilla bands annoyed him greatly. They interfered with traffic along the Mississippi River south of Memphis and along the line of the Memphis & Charleston Railroad east of Memphis.

General William T. Sherman. Sherman called his Meridian Campaign a "pleasant excursion," but he waited in vain in the ruins of Meridian for Smith. *Photograph taken from* The Photographic History of the Civil War in Ten Volumes, *ed. Francis Trevelyan Miller, vol. 10.*

Two months before the fall of Vicksburg, Union General William Sooy Smith[21] had tangled with one of the most bothersome of these small commands, "Sol Street's Guerilla Band." Smith charged that Street had murdered two of his men, and he threatened reprisals.[22] In his book *Sherman's Mississippi Campaign*, Buck Foster showed that Sherman believed there was no solution to the problem of guerilla activity short of bringing "hard war" to Mississippi; i.e., taking harsh reprisals against private property on both banks of the river south of Memphis. By January, he concluded that these measures had succeeded there and could be applied elsewhere.

The railroad line east of Memphis also troubled Sherman. It attracted Confederate guerilla bands, sometimes joined by regular cavalry forces. Collierville, just to the east of Memphis, was a favorite target in the fall of 1863. On October 11, General James Chalmers attacked the Union camp there just as a train bearing Sherman and his staff, bound for Corinth, neared the station. The Confederates attacked the train, destroyed the locomotive and seized the rear car. Sherman lost his horse, sword and spare uniform. The fighting lasted several hours. Union casualties were just under one hundred, and Confederate losses were about half that.[23]

Sherman was determined to put an end to all of these raids, but his ambition went further than securing the railroad. He was willing to give up posts along the railroad, including even Corinth, if he could embark on the larger project of bringing "hard war" to Mississippi.

In the Vicksburg campaign, Sherman had seen the Union army forage in the countryside through which it passed, doing without a fixed and lengthening line of supply. To that he now meant to add a heavy punitive expedition, bringing the destructive effects of war to the civilian population. Such tactics would deny support to guerilla bands and deny supplies of corn to major armies. It would also have a destructive effect on civilian morale. To be sure, the invaders were to distinguish between public property essential to the South's war-making ability and private property that could not be so construed. But this was a theoretical distinction only, as Sherman well knew. Regretfully (he claimed), he noted how difficult it was to enforce such a theoretical distinction.[24] In any case, the goal of destruction—crippling Confederate strategy for the spring of 1864—far outweighed such scruples. He aimed to bring about "the most complete destruction of railroads ever beheld."[25] He had contemplated such a bold, heavy stroke ever since Vicksburg fell. "You will remember," he wrote Major General U.S. Grant, then commander of the Military Division of the Mississippi, in March 1864, "when in July last Vicksburg surrendered and a detachment of the

Army of the Tennessee under my command had pushed the rebel army under General Johnston into and beyond Jackson, it was the purpose to go on eastward and destroy the remaining railroads of the state in and near Meridian."[26] Sherman had wanted to get underway as soon as possible.

But then, suddenly and unexpectedly, a problem arose. After the fall of Chattanooga in early September, Union General William Rosecrans believed that Bragg's Army of Tennessee would retreat all the way to Dalton, Georgia. It did not. Instead, Bragg lay in wait just south of Chattanooga, where he was reinforced from the Army of Northern Virginia. On September 20, 1864, Bragg attacked Rosecrans's force along Chickamauga Creek and won a great victory. The Confederates drove Rosecrans back into the defenses of Chattanooga. Although some of Bragg's officers, including General Nathan Bedford Forrest, urged Bragg to follow up the victory with an immediate attack on Rosecrans's defeated force, Bragg chose instead to lay siege to the city. Chickamauga was, in that sense, a hollow victory, but it called for Grant's attention and presence. Chickamauga forestalled any operations in Mississippi of the magnitude Sherman envisioned. Thus he fretted and chafed with inactivity during the summer and fall. He wanted his infantry in the field. He knew, or thought he knew, that troops held too long in a city like Memphis become enervated.[27] But he was forced to wait.

In November, the situation changed again, this time favorably for the Union. Grant raised the siege of Chattanooga, driving the Confederates off Lookout Mountain and Missionary Ridge (November 24–25). The Army of Tennessee did now retreat to Dalton, Georgia, where General Joseph E. Johnston replaced Bragg in command.

Chattanooga was now safe for the Union, but Atlanta might not be for the Confederacy. And the next reinforcements for the Army of Tennessee might have to come from Mississippi. In any event, Sherman seized on the interval between December 1863 and the spring campaign of 1864: the "time and an opportunity were offered to accomplish what had before been designed…to attempt the destruction of Meridian without calling for a single man from the army in the field."[28] He had twenty thousand infantry as a nucleus: four divisions of the XVI and XVII Corps, the former under Major General James McPherson, at Vicksburg, and the latter under Major General Benjamin Hurlbut, at Memphis. On January 10, Sherman wrote to McPherson, saying, "Now is the time to strike inland at Meridian and Selma. I think Vicksburg is the point of departure from the river."[29]

A few days later he expanded on his plan, adding a diversion north from the Gulf and a cavalry thrust south from Memphis. On January 14, he wrote to General Nathaniel P. Banks, commanding the Department of the Gulf at New Orleans, about a possible feint toward Mobile Bay to hold Confederate forces there as he neared Meridian.[30] On the same day, he told General Henry Halleck in Washington that he would have cavalry coming down the Mobile & Ohio toward Meridian to meet him there.[31]

By January 15, Grant had approved Sherman's plan, and so informed General Halleck. Sherman would collect at Vicksburg all available forces for a movement across the state to Jackson and then Meridian. He had given Sherman "large discretionary powers" to decide whether to go beyond Meridian or return to Vicksburg. In any event, the destruction he would inflict will be of "material importance to us in preventing the enemy from drawing supplies from Mississippi and in clearing that section of all large bodies of rebel troops."[32]

As Sherman set about making his final arrangements, he learned that General William Sooy Smith, Grant's chief of cavalry, was to command of the cavalry force that would meet him in Meridian. Sherman did not think that Smith was the right man for the task. Smith was then at Corinth with six cavalry regiments, about 2,500 men. He reported to Grant on January 12 that he was "now collecting all the cavalry we can get hold of in West Tennessee" to take part in Sherman's Meridian expedition. Smith envisioned a force of 6,500 cavalry, which he thought was "ample." He mentioned General Nathan B. Forrest twice in his dispatch. Forrest was no longer with the Army of Tennessee. In December, he had gone into west Tennessee to recruit a new cavalry command. Smith had been among the Union cavalrymen trying in vain to trap him there. Smith noted Forrest's escape, adding that he was "anxious to attack him [Forrest] at once, but General Sherman thinks I had better await his movement, and in the mean time collect, organize, and supply my command."[33]

Smith had Grant's full confidence and, very likely, that of Major General Hurlbut, the Memphis commander, but he did not have Sherman's. In December, he had expressed misgivings about Smith to Grant: "I deem General W. Sooy Smith is too mistrustful of himself for a leader against Forrest."[34] Later, in April, he commented: "I had not the selection of Genl. Wm. Sooy Smith. General Grant selected him after a long personal and official association."[35]

If Sherman did not think highly of Smith, it also seems that he regarded Forrest as only a disagreeable nuisance and not a formidable opponent. In his memoirs, published in 1876, Sherman wrote that "a chief part of the enterprise was to destroy the rebel cavalry commanded by Forrest...I wanted to destroy General Forrest."[36] At the time, however, Sherman did not seem to understand the quality of man Smith might encounter. In September 1863, he had contemptuously described Forrest, John Hunt Morgan and J.E.B. Stuart as no more than "splendid riders, shots, and utterly reckless" men who must be "killed or employed by us before we can hope for peace."[37] Now, on January 11, he spoke of Forrest in the same breath as the guerilla leaders, the "Mounted Devils" and "wandering Arabs" about whom "I am sure all we can do is to make the country feel that the people must pay."[38] Sherman later spoke of Forrest in blood-curdling tones, but at the time he seems to have underestimated him. It was not likely, however, as Sherman speculated in late January 1864, "that Forrest will let Smith pass down and make a dash for Memphis."[39] As the date for the campaign approached, Sherman became more cautionary, warning Smith about Forrest's energy.

With less than full confidence in Smith, Sherman set him a very difficult task. Meridian is 230 miles from Smith's point of departure, which proved to be Collierville, Tennessee, near Memphis—a trip that can take four and a half hours today. Sherman may have found some assurance in the fact that Colonel Grierson would ride with Smith as a *de facto* second-in-command. Later, Grierson claimed that Sherman promised to put him in command once the force joined the infantry at Meridian. Smith would then be bundled back to Collierville.[40]

Smith was born in Tarleton, Ohio, on July 33, 1830. Though Quakers, his grandfather and father served in the Revolutionary War and the War of 1812, respectively. As a youth and college student, he worked as a janitor on the Ohio University campus in Athens, Ohio, to earn his tuition. He was known as "Professor of Dust and Ashes." He graduated in 1849 and went on to West Point. Oliver Otis Howard, later a Union general, knew him there as "a professing Christian."[41] He graduated from West Point in 1853, sixth in his class, twenty-eight positions above that of another later Union cavalryman, Phillip H. Sheridan.[42] Smith soon resigned to begin a career as a civil engineer. Among other projects, he made the first surveys for the International Bridge at Niagara Falls. In 1857, he became chief engineer at the Trenton Locomotive Works. When war came, he volunteered and served first as assistant adjutant general at Camp Dennison, Ohio. He was promoted to colonel, commanding the 13th Ohio Volunteers. In April 1862, he was promoted again, to brigadier general. By the time he came to Sherman, he had served in West Virginia and at Shiloh and Perryville. He also showed an engineer's aptitude for military railroad work—building blockhouses, stockades and probably bridges. Later, he claimed credit for the idea of

Colonel Benjamin Grierson (far right). Grierson was a successful and experienced cavalry raider, but he accompanied Smith's force without a formal command. *Photograph taken from* The Photographic History of the Civil War in Ten Volumes, *ed. Francis Trevelyan Miller, vol. 4.*

launching Grierson's Raid, so destructive of railroads. He commanded a diversionary column in that raid (April 17–21, 1863), but saw little action.[43] At the end of 1862, he was transferred to Grant's command and took over the First Division of the XVI Corps. His monumental bust stands today at the Vicksburg National Military Park. After the fall of Vicksburg, Grant appointed him his chief of cavalry.[44] In December and January 1864, Smith had been among the cavalry commanders who tried to trap Forrest, recruiting behind Union lines in West Tennessee.

General William Sooy Smith. Smith was a successful civil engineer before and after the Civil War, credited with building the first steel railroad bridge, over the Mississippi River at Glasgow, Missouri. *Photograph taken from* The Photographic History of the Civil War in Ten Volumes, *ed. Francis Trevelyan Miller, vol. 10.*

Smith's record raises some question about experience—he had never commanded a cavalry force larger than the six regiments he had in Corinth in January 1864. But the most striking question his record raises is about his health. He lived a long life—until 1916—but in 1864, at thirty-four years of age, he had a troubling medical record. His early career in engineering "was interrupted by a desperate illness." His wife's care may have saved his life. He had gone on sick leave after Shiloh and again in December 1862. He was sick again during the Vicksburg Campaign.[45] Commanders often have to compensate for relative inexperience and grow into their commands and responsibilities, but Smith may have been simply not up to the rigor of a cavalry operation in Mississippi.

After meeting with Smith for the first time on January 10, 1864, Sherman assembled for him a force of unprecedented strength. He increased Smith's force to about seven thousand men. He ordered Colonel George E. Waring's brigade, then near Columbus, Kentucky, to join Smith at Collierville. Waring began his march of over 160 miles on January 22. Like Smith, Waring's background was in engineering. He was a drainage engineer and an agricultural chemist. He had served with the 4th Missouri Cavalry since 1861.[46] His march to Collierville proved unexpectedly difficult. No one foresaw how long it would take Waring to cross the Obion and Wolf Rivers and countless other streams. Swollen streams "delayed us long with torrents of bottomless muddy water…rough, rocky, wooded country."[47] It would take Waring eighteen days to complete his march. His regiments did not begin coming in to Collierville until February 8.

Once assembled, Smith's force was a powerful one. A modern historian, Margie Bearss, noted that "up to this stage of the Civil War, this was the largest cavalry command to undertake a raid."[48] However, the long delay in bringing the force together seriously jeopardized the spirit and letter of Sherman's orders to Smith.

SMITH'S COMMAND, FEBRUARY 1864[49]

FIRST BRIGADE—COLONEL GEORGE E. WARING JR.

2nd Illinois (5 companies)	Capt. Franklin Moore
7th Indiana	Col. John Shanks
4th Missouri (U.S.)	Major Gustav Heinrichs
3rd New Jersey	Capt. Joseph Karge'
19th Pennsylvania	Major Amos Holahan

SECOND BRIGADE—LIEUTENANT COLONEL WILLIAM P. HEPBURN

6th Illinois	Lt. Col. Mathew Stair
7th Illinois	Lt. Col. George W. Trafton
9th Illinois	Lt. Col. Henry B. Burgh
1st Illinois Light Artillery Battery K	Lt. Isaac W. Curtis

THIRD BRIGADE—COLONEL LAFAYETTE MCCRILLIS

3rd Illinois (5 companies)	Capt. Andrew B. Kirkbride
72nd Indiana (mounted infantry)	Major Henry M. Carr
5th Kentucky (U.S.)	Major Christopher T. Cheek
2nd Tennessee (U.S.)	Lt. Col. William. R. Cook
3rd Tennessee (U.S.)	Major John D. Minnis
4th Tennessee (U.S.)	Lt. Col. Jacob M. Thornburgh

UNATTACHED

4th U.S. Regulars	Capt. Charles S. Bowman

Sherman had never been certain that Smith could move fast enough to suit him. On January 24, he seemed to suggest to Grant that he would set Smith in motion from Memphis *before* he himself set out from Vicksburg.[50] He then changed his mind. He later reported to Grant that he ordered Smith "to move from Memphis by or before the 1st of February with an effective force of 7,000 cavalry, lightly equipped, to march straight on Pontotoc, Okolona, Columbus Junction (Artesia), and Meridian, to arrive there about February 10."[51] In special field orders issued on January 27, Sherman laid out the basic themes for the campaign, stressing above all that "the expedition is one of celerity and all things must tend to that." Special instructions to Smith then followed. In these he did not specifically cite February 1 as Smith's departure date, but his meaning was clear. He told Smith he meant to be in Meridian with four infantry divisions by February 10, and then this: "I want you with your cavalry to march from Collierville on Pontotoc and Okolona, thence sweeping down the Mobile & Ohio Railroad…and finally reach me at or near Meridian as near the date I have mentioned as possible." He went on: "This will call for great energy of action on your part, but I believe you are up to it and you have the best and most experienced troops in the service, and they will do anything that is possible. General Grierson is with you and is familiar with the whole country…I wish you to attack any force of cavalry you meet and follow them southward, but in no event be drawn into the forks of the Yazoo, nor over into Alabama. Do not let the enemy draw you into minor affairs, but look solely to the greater object to destroy his communications from Okolona to Meridian and thence eastward to Selma. From Okolona south you will find abundance of forage collected along the railroad, and the farms have standing cover in the fields. Take liberally of all there, as well as horses, mules, cattle, etc. As a rule respect dwelling and families…but mills, barns, sheds, stables and such like things use for the benefit and convenience of your command. If convenient send into Columbus and destroy all the machinery there and the bridge across the Tombigbee…we have talked over this matter so much that the above covers all points not provided for in my published orders of today."[52]

Sherman's directives left little or no room for misunderstanding. But they also left no room for the "friction" of war—the unforeseen events that often rise up in the face of armies once the wheels have begun to turn. Although Smith's force appeared to be both large and powerful, with clear orders in hand, difficulties arose almost immediately. As early as January 2, General Hurlbut had warned Sherman that all the cavalry in the department were "wearing out from hard service…and I cannot procure a remount."[53] In his dispatch to Grant on January 12, Smith had gone on at great length about the bad condition of his horses.[54] Evidently, the situation did not improve over the next five days. On January 17, Smith wrote Grant again: "Since my arrival here I have been working away with all my might to get the cavalry of this district into effective condition…nearly all the cavalry…needed a great deal of shoeing after racing about after Forrest…as soon as I can get our cavalry together and in shape I will attack him…General Sherman desires me to sweep down toward Columbus and Meridian…on this account our delay in preparation is less irksome."[55]

A dispatch to Sherman on January 28 reveals an even more uneasy combination of fading bravado and looming worry: "Information just received indicates a movement of Forrest's command to Oxford. They have information of our intentions…I think Forrest will endeavor to cover the Mobile & Ohio Railroad. I will pitch into him wherever I find him. The cavalry from Columbus has not yet arrived."[56]

Smith's commitment to the campaign, and perhaps his will to action, seemed to be crumbling. "Exceedingly chagrined," Smith wrote Sherman on February 4 to say that because "in our conversations a force of 7,000 was always hypothecated I feel in doubt as to what you would direct me to do if you were here…I feel eager to pitch into them but I know that it is not your desire to 'send a boy to mill.'" He continued in the same disconcerted tone, saying that if he met Forrest around Ripley [!] "it would suit us much better than to fight him as low down as Pontotoc, where he could accumulate a larger force and where we would be to some extent jaded and further from home." Facing up to it with an almost audible deep breath, Smith declared that if he had not heard from Colonel Waring's brigade by the next day [February 3], "I will move down and try what I can do with what I have." Smith then hastened to add that in addition to Forrest's command, he would likely face Wheeler's cavalry as well.[57]

Smith wrote Sherman in fine fettle on February 10, in a dispatch that Sherman almost certainly never saw. Waring's brigade had arrived the previous day; Smith had moved an infantry brigade toward Panola to draw attention away from his movement toward New Albany. He regretted being late—it was "unavoidable by any effort I could make"—but his command was in "splendid condition." The Confederates under Forrest were waiting for him "in force…but I will hurt them all I can…weather beautiful, roads getting good."[58]

Waring's force reached Smith between February 8 and February 10, the day the force was to have been in Meridian. On February 11, Smith confessed to Grant, "I have worried myself into a state of morbid anxiety that I will be entirely too late."[59]

Chapter 3

"Forrest's Cavalry Department"

In the late summer of 1863, the Confederate high command became concerned about the safety of the Mississippi Prairie. With the Confederacy contracting into the Deep South and Virginia, rich and fertile areas like the Shenandoah Valley and the Mississippi Prairie became even more important. The commanding officer in Columbus, General Daniel Ruggles, called the Prairie "about the best grain producing portion of the state." He thought that cavalry units could not provide protection enough to satisfy the region's planters, and he recommended "that one well disciplined regiment of Confederate troops be sent here for service at or in advance of Okolona."[60]

The Prairie was now part of General Leonidas Polk's Department of Alabama, Mississippi and East Louisiana. On August 18, Polk was glad to see Major General Stephen D. Lee take up command of Confederate cavalry in Mississippi. Lee had a distinguished record in the Army of Northern Virginia and in the defense of Vicksburg. "General Lee is a fighting general and will keep the cavalry busy for the winter," wrote one Confederate.[61]

With good reason, Sherman thought that Lee was "the most enterprising of all in their army" at Vicksburg. In December 1862, Lee and General Carter Stevenson had inflicted over two thousand casualties on Sherman at the Battle of Chickasaw Bayou, above Vicksburg. Lee was among the Confederates taken prisoner when the garrison surrendered. He was later paroled. Sherman hoped that a way could be found to disqualify Lee from service in Mississippi,[62] but Lee's parole was in order.

General Stephen D. Lee. His legacies include the Vicksburg National Park, Mississippi A&M College (now Mississippi State University) and the United Confederate Veterans (now the Sons of Confederate Veterans). Painted by John Slato, from the original (1877) by Nicola Marschall. *Courtesy of the Stephen Dill Lee Home and Museum, Columbus, Mississippi. Photograph by Elisa Shizak.*

His first task in Mississippi was to set his command in order. It was fortunate for Lee that Sherman had not been able to advance into Mississippi in the summer of 1863. The following dispatch, which Lee may have seen, reveals some of the problems he faced as commander. Colonel R.V. Richardson, commanding a small force at New Albany in October 1863, wrote to a quartermaster officer: "If I am to protect this district and the Mobile & Ohio Railroad you must give me more men, equipment and ammunition. I do not have a single vessel to cook one morsel of bread…I want clothing, shoes and blankets…I say again, send me skillets…I cannot fight any more until I get something to cook in."[63]

On September 1, Lee completed a comprehensive report on his command. "This command is generally not in good condition…the line now being protected is a very long one and difficult one to protect successfully." He noted, as had General Ruggles, the "bad political feeling" in north Mississippi, adding that "in raids of the enemy many of the partisan and state troops disperse." There had not been a "proper understanding between the Confederate and state authorities" in the past. Beyond that, there were simply too many small, untrained cavalry commands in north Mississippi, "all brought about by ambitious men striving for command and position." There were too many commands with too few horses and too little discipline. But he did see some signs of hope. The fighting at Chattanooga and in north Georgia gave him some time, at least, to set his command to rights. He believed that a strong recruiting effort—behind Union lines in west Tennessee—would replenish his ranks. He wrote, "I visited Colonel Richardson's command from West Tennessee…near Okolona. He has authority from the War Department to raise troops in West Tennessee...the Colonel had about 600 men with him...he has about 2,000 stands of arms...he expects more men to come from West Tennessee in a few days."[64]

Above all else, however, Lee needed an experienced officer who could implement his wishes, a man whose presence would inspire confidence among soldiers and civilians alike. Lee knew of such an officer, then with the Army of Tennessee. He had seen "several newspaper allusions" to this officer's imminent resignation from that army. On November 6, he wrote to army headquarters, then near Chattanooga: "I would respectfully state that, if any local causes exist in the Army of Tennessee against General Forrest remaining there, that there is a good field for his labors in West Tennessee, where his popularity would enable him to raise at least 4,000 men."[65]

Nathan Bedford Forrest was forty-two in 1864. His reputation then was not yet of mythic proportions, but he was without a doubt a remarkable and formidable man. Completely without military experience or training, he entered the Confederate service as an enlisted man and finished the war as a lieutenant general—the only man on either side to attain that rank without military experience.

The contrast between Forrest and his (soon-to-be) adversary, William Sooy Smith, is very sharp. Smith was both a college and West Point graduate and a successful engineer. Forrest had no—or very little—education. His career had been in cotton, slaves, Coahoma County (Mississippi) real estate and Memphis politics. Forrest was well connected, particularly with Tennessee's governor Isham Harris, but rough-hewn. He had killed a man before the war in the town square of Hernando, Mississippi.[66] He relished personal combat. Like Smith, Forrest was an early volunteer. Forrest had all the characteristics of a compelling and effective leader. He was selflessly dedicated to the cause of Southern independence. He was single-minded, clearheaded, tireless and physically strong. He led by personal example, inspiring others to go beyond themselves. His knowledge of Tennessee, Mississippi and Alabama was firsthand and deep. He had an aura of authority blended with a common touch. Above all, he had the aura of success. By 1864, he had already raised and equipped two separate commands, largely at his own expense. He had led detached commands, raiding behind enemy lines and repelling enemy raids. But he had also served with the Army of Tennessee under Albert Sydney Johnston at Shiloh and under Braxton Bragg at Chickamauga. In the Army of Tennessee, he had held regimental, brigade, division and corps command.

Two episodes in particular revealed his resourcefulness, energy and ferocious determination. In February 1862, he refused to follow his craven superior officers in surrendering their commands to General Grant at Fort Donelson. Instead, he led his command out of the doomed fort at night. It was an important turning point, away from months of captivity toward greatness in the field.

In late April 1863 he relentlessly pursued Colonel Abel Streight's raiding force across Alabama before finally forcing it to surrender near Rome, Georgia, on May 2, 1863. Dispatches from Forrest in his own verbiage, rather than that of an aide, are exceedingly rare. The one he sent on to Rome during his pursuit of Streight may be the only extant example. It gives a good impression of the man and his relentless and tireless nature. "Prepare your selves to Repuls them—they have 2 Mountain howitzers. I will be close on them. I have kild 300 of their men. they air running for their lives."[67]

As a raider, he had few equals. He led two successful forays into west Tennessee, one in July and one in December 1862. In the latter raid, he destroyed railroad lines and supply depots around Jackson, Tennessee, helping to cripple Grant's Vicksburg campaign of that year. He had survived two serious wounds, and had been promoted to major general (December 4, 1862). On the battlefield, he had a ringing voice that roared above the clash and mayhem of battle. "I'll swear I never heard such a voice. It penetrated you through and through and made you move," wrote one officer.[68] One observer described him in early 1864: "He was well mounted and wore a shiny black hat such as the Blockade Runners bring through from Memphis and sell at $80—he had a pretty good uniform except the hat; he must be at least six feet in height...he seldom smiled and is said never to laugh...he is what the ladies would call a handsome man."[69] Another Confederate wrote that Forrest's "presence seemed to inspire everyone with his terrible energy, which was more like that of a piece of powerful steam machinery than of a human being."[70] "His visage," said another Confederate, "said to all the world 'Out of my way, I'm coming.'"[71]

Forrest's men had seen hard fighting by 1864, both mounted and on foot. Forrest had learned the effectiveness of fighting men dismounted as a kind of mobile infantry. Later, European military writers credited him with a great innovation, or timely revival of a past practice, in leading cavalry into battle as "mounted rifles or mounted infantry."[72] With their long rifles and varied headgear, Forrest's men even looked like infantry. At Chickamauga, Lieutenant General D.H. Hill, in command of an infantry corps, saw Forrest's men going into action and asked, "What infantry is that?"[73]

His artillery commander, John Morton, wrote that his chief "cared nothing for tactics further than movement by twos or fours in column right or left into line, dismounting, charging and fighting…except for officers, as an insignia of rank, General Forrest banished the saber from his command. He armed his men with Sharps rifles, or short carbines, and two Navy Sixes."[74]

General Bragg spoke highly of Forrest—before Chickamauga. In the unfortunate aftermath of that hollow victory, however, Forrest was one of several high-ranking officers Bragg wanted to be rid of. General St. John Liddell recalled Bragg's complaint: "I have not a single general officer of cavalry fit for command…look at Forrest! The man is ignorant and does not know anything of cooperation. He is nothing more than a good raider."[75]

Although Forrest had hoped for a transfer to Mississippi, even before Chickamauga, he was not among the twelve signers of a petition circulated in the army's high command urging President Davis to remove Bragg. The petition prompted President Davis to visit army headquarters on Missionary Ridge (October 9), but by that time Bragg had already stripped Forrest of his command and had placed him under the command of General Joseph Wheeler. By some (undocumented) accounts, a furious Forrest resigned his commission. In another account, that of his physician Dr. Cowan, Forrest vented his fury in a personal confrontation with Bragg. What is certain is that by October 14, when the president left army headquarters, Bragg would remain in command but Forrest, Polk and other officers would no longer serve in the Army of Tennessee. Later in the month (October 27 or 28), Forrest met with President Davis in Montgomery. The result of their meeting was that Forrest headed west for what became informally known as "Forrest's Cavalry Department" in east Mississippi and east Tennessee. He would serve under General Stephen D. Lee and the department commander General Polk. He brought with him barely three hundred men. For the third time in his career, he had to recruit his new command, this time from behind Federal lines in west Tennessee.[76] As Trooper Dinkins noted, "Forrest now entered upon a new epoch in his military career."[77]

Lee could not have been more pleased. On November 7, he sent Forrest a most cordial letter of welcome: "No longer ago than yesterday I wrote General Bragg stating that if you were unpleasantly situated, West Tennessee offered a good field and that Richardson's brigade in North Mississippi… would be a nucleus for you to build a large command…whether you are under my command or not, we shall not disagree, and you shall have all the assistance and support I can render you. I would feel proud either in commanding or cooperating with so gallant an officer as yourself."[78]

Forrest established temporary headquarters at Okolona. He had about eight hundred men: some of Colonel Richardson's command, the three hundred or so men who had been allotted to him from the Army of Tennessee, his staff, his Escort, another small battalion of cavalry and Morton's Battery. Arms and horses were in short supply.[79] He had a good nucleus for a command but lacked the numerical strength for effective combat. He needed recruits. He knew he could find them in west Tennessee. According to General Chalmers, soon to be Forrest's second-in-command, "At this time west Tennessee was full of little companies of from 10 to 30 men willing to fight but unwilling to go far from home or into the infantry service."[80] The problem was getting into and then out of west Tennessee. Numerous streams, beginning with the Tallahatchie in north Mississippi, barred his path. There was also the fortified line of the Memphis & Charleston Railroad, running east from Memphis. Not least of his problems was the great distance to be traveled; New Albany, where he would likely cross the Tallahatchie, was nearly one hundred miles from Jackson, Tennessee, where he would establish another temporary headquarters. The terrain was rough, and the winter was already unusually and extremely cold.

Forrest sent Colonel Tyree Bell and other officers well known in west Tennessee ahead of the main body. He followed from Okolona on December 1 with about 450 men. Lee accompanied him with some of his command. They went up the Pontotoc Road and then to Ripley, where the two commands diverged—Lee to make a diversionary attack to create an opening for Forrest to cross the patrolled railroad line. Forrest crossed the line without incident near Grand Junction, Tennessee, and reached Jackson, Tennessee, on December 4. He immediately issued a call for recruits. Some men he conscripted.[81] The results were as Chalmers had predicted. One volunteer wrote, "I determined to cast my fortunes with the daring and dashing Forrest...he was constantly receiving recruits...wherever he went many old, seasoned, wounded soldiers joined him from choice."[82] On December 8, Forrest sent dispatches to the War Department and to Generals Bragg and Lee: "I am highly gratified with my success so far and with the prospects...troops and men are flocking to me in all quarters."[83]

By the day before Christmas in 1863, his time in west Tennessee was nearly up. Federal forces were converging on him, fifteen thousand strong. Reluctantly, Forrest decided to leave behind some of the unarmed men who had come in, but he brought the greater number south with him. He returned to Mississippi with a force six times larger than that he had brought to Tennessee. A correspondent for the *Cincinnati Commercial* well described Forrest's exploit:

Major General James A. Chalmers. Chalmers commanded the District of Mississippi and East Louisiana before he became Forrest's subordinate. Nevertheless, the two cooperated successfully. *Photograph taken from* The Photographic History of the Civil War in Ten Volumes, *ed. Francis Trevelyan Miller, vol. 4.*

"Forrest, with less than 1000 men, has moved right through the Sixteenth Army Corps, has passed within nine miles of Memphis, carried off over 100 wagons, 200 beef cattle, 3000 conscripts and innumerable stores…and are too in the face of 10,000 men."[84]

Forrest rested his command at Mount Pleasant, near Holly Springs, on December 28, and then moved to Como. At Como, he set about transforming his band of men into a fighting force.[85] It would be no easy task. "I have nevertheless 3100 new troops and hope soon to do good service with them," he wrote.[86] He seemed to have more officers than privates, all representing "odds and ends of paper commands," as he put it to President Davis. Some skeleton units were dissolved, while others were merged. For example, Forrest merged Sol Street's band, which had joined him in Tennessee, with the 15th and 16th Tennessee to form a new 15th Tennessee. The former partisan leader was now Major Street. Together with other partisans, Street became an effective officer and a "good hand" under Forrest. Forrest relied heavily on Colonel Bell; together they "worked furiously to whip the brigade and the little army into shape." One of his Escort wrote in his diary, "A drill nearly every day."[87] Forrest proved himself an effective, if unpolished, orator, often exhorting the men in evening reviews, "which stirs greatly," one soldier wrote.[88]

In the middle of the month, Forrest traveled to Jackson, Mississippi, to meet with General Polk. Very soon thereafter, arms and ammunition began to arrive in Como.[89] By the end of January, Forrest had completed his organization. His force was now made up of four small brigades, commanded by General Bell, Colonel Richardson, Colonel Robert ("Black Bob") McCulloch and Colonel Jeffery Forrest. The latter two brigades formed a division under Colonel Chalmers, now Forrest's second-in-command. Captain John Morton commanded the artillery—Thrall's, Rice's and Hoole's Batteries. Captain Thomas Tate led Forrest's Escort.

FORREST'S COMMAND, JANUARY 25, 1864[90]

FIRST BRIGADE—BRIGADIER GENERAL R.V. RICHARDSON

12th Tennessee Cavalry Regiment	Lt. Col. J.U. Green
14th Tennessee Cavalry Regiment	Col. J.J. Neely
15th Tennessee Cavalry Regiment	Col. F.M. Stewart
16th Tennessee Cavalry Regiment	Col. T.H. Logwood
17th Tennessee Cavalry Regiment	Major Marshal
Street's Battalion	
Bennett's Battalion	

Total: 1,500 men

SECOND BRIGADE—COLONEL ROBERT MCCULLOCH

2nd Missouri Cavalry Regiment	Col. Robert McCulloch
Willis's Texas Battalion	Lt. Col. Lee Willis
Faulkner's Kentucky Regiment	Col. W.W. Faulkner
Keiser's and Franklin's Tennessee Battalion	Lt. Col. Alexander
Mississippi Cavalry Battalion	Lt. Col. Alexander Chalmers
2nd Arkansas Cavalry (fragment)	Captain F.M. Cochran

Total: strength not given

THIRD BRIGADE—COLONEL T. H. BELL

* Note: The Third and Fourth Brigades were a demi-division commanded by General James Chalmers

Col. Russell's Tennessee Regiment	
Col. Greer's Tennessee Regiment	
Col. Newsom's Tennessee Regiment	
Col. Wilson's Tennessee Regiment	
2nd Tennessee Cavalry Regiment	Major C.R. Barteau

Total: 2,000 men

FOURTH BRIGADE—COLONEL JEFFREY FORREST

* Note: The Third and Fourth Brigades were a demi-division commanded by General James Chalmers

McDonald's Battalion	Major Charles McDonald
7th Tennessee Cavalry Regiment	Lt. Col. Duckworth
McGuirk's Regiment	
3rd Mississippi State Troops	
5th Mississippi Cavalry Regiment	Lt. Col. Barksdale
Duff's (19th) Mississippi Battalion	

Total: strength not given

"Forrest's Cavalry Department"

ARTILLERY—CAPTAIN JOHN MORTON
Thrall's Battery
Rice's Battery
Hoole's Battery

FORREST'S ESCORT—CAPTAIN THOMAS TATE

There was both strength and flexibility in his order of battle, but he was painfully aware of how small his force was and how important it was to keep the men he had. The plague of desertion ran high among officers and men alike, especially after February 2, when Forrest moved the command to Oxford. On February 10, Escort trooper William Dyer noted in his diary that the Escort had been sent out after a group of men headed for home and had brought them back to Oxford. On February 12, nineteen men stood condemned as deserters, faced a firing squad. Forrest had ordered their execution and adamantly refused pleas for mercy, including those from clergymen in town. The nineteen men stood before their open graves—until Forrest pardoned them, literally at the last moment. His mercy hung by a thread but his decision was wise. He would need every man now, and the spirit of all.[91] The defense of the Prairie was in his hands alone.

The new year, 1864, would prove to be the most terrible year of the war, even though its bloodiest day, at Sharpsburg, and its bloodiest battle, at Gettysburg, were already in the past. The fighting in 1864 was ferocious and, above all, sustained, almost unremitting. The Confederacy, reeling from the terrible summer of 1863, found itself under tremendous and simultaneous pressure everywhere. Charleston Harbor remained under siege. The Gulf Coast, particularly Mobile, became a target. Union operations in Louisiana along the Red River began in late May. Everywhere, casualties rose to unprecedented figures. Both sides fought with desperate determination. There was a presidential election coming in the North, but there was no political solution for the Confederacy. For the South, there was no turning back. As the Confederacy shrank, the fighting took on a more bitter tone. On February 17, the Confederate submarine *Hunley* sank a Union warship in Charleston Harbor. Three days later, a Union punitive and destructive expedition similar to Sherman's and Smith's came to grief with the Confederate victory at Olustee. There were nearly two thousand casualties. But the first major army to move in 1864 was Sherman's. There was no heavy fighting on the march between Vicksburg and Meridian, but Sherman's swath of destruction marked the new tone of the new year's war.

Sherman's compatriot, Smith, did face heavy opposition in the Prairie.

Forrest was now ready. On the last day of January, Dyer wrote in his diary, "Everything was active. Man and horse in good condition—orders to prepare for a march."[92] Sherman marched from Vicksburg on February 2. What General Stephen D. Lee called the "Sherman torch" was about to set the Prairie ablaze.[93]

Nathan Bedford Forrest, now entering the worst year of the war, was beginning his greatest year as a soldier.

Chapter 4

"I Think They Are Badly Scared"

We will take all provisions and God help the starving families.
—*William T. Sherman, January 28, 1864*[94]

We are pretty near the end of the struggle.
—Mobile Advertiser & Register, *February 3, 1864*[95]

S herman began the Meridian campaign on February 3–4, 1864, setting
out from Vicksburg with over twenty thousand men, aiming for Jackson
and then Meridian. At the same time, Union gunboats and troop transports
pushed up the Yazoo River from Vicksburg, heading for Yazoo City. At
Collierville, east of Memphis, Smith's two cavalry brigades remained in their
camps, waiting for the arrival of Waring's brigade. At his headquarters in
Oxford, Forrest learned of Sherman's departure from General Polk, who was
at his departmental headquarters in Meridian. Most of Forrest's men were
along the south bank of the Tallahatchie; the largest part, under Chalmers,
was at Panola, about thirty-five miles west and north of Oxford. They
could be moved to support whatever forces Polk could bring to bear against
Sherman. But Forrest was watching Memphis. Thanks to Captain Thomas
Henderson's Confederate scouts, Forrest had known since January 11 that
Union cavalry were concentrating near Memphis, although Henderson did
not learn their plans.

In his Collierville camps, Smith passed the first days of February
waiting for his missing brigade and fretting over supplies for his men and

horses. Waring's regiments did not begin coming in until February 8. They had come a great distance under trying conditions and were worn down and short of supplies and ammunition. Things had gone awry at the very beginning. Sherman's expectation was that Smith would join him at Meridian on or about February 10. Sherman did not get there until February 14, but Smith's force did not get underway from Collierville until February 10–11. Colonel LaFayette McCrillis's Third Brigade led the way, followed by Lieutenant Colonel William Hepburn's Second Brigade. Waring's brigade was the last to leave, delayed again by the late arrival of a train bringing sorely needed supplies.

Once in motion, Smith planned to cross the Tallahatchie at New Albany and then head for the Prairie and the Mobile & Ohio. To divert Confederate attention from his New Albany crossing, he sent General William McMillan's infantry brigade, assigned to him for this purpose, to approach the Tallahatchie at Wyatt, west of New Albany. McMillan passed through Hernando and Senatobia before reaching Wyatt. On February 7, Forrest had ordered Colonel Forrest's brigade to Grenada, and then went himself with Bell's brigade, but Smith's attempted diversion did not mislead him. Late on February 9, he notified Chalmers, still at Panola, "I am of the opinion the real move is in the direction of Okolona and Meridian." And then, "Do not allow your command to engage a superior force." He ordered his brother's brigade to push hard from Grenada east to West Point, and ordered Chalmers east as well. By February 17, Chalmers was east of Houston, entering the Prairie. Forrest was at Starkville on February 18. Colonel Forrest had gone on from West Point and was watching the Prairie from the direction of Aberdeen and Prairie Station.[96]

Meanwhile, Smith moved his brigades by different routes toward New Albany. Their movements were difficult to coordinate. Unfairly, perhaps, and in retrospect, Smith's subordinates complained about what they perceived as a lack of direction and purpose. Waring wrote, "We marched in three columns over different roads, each for himself, with only a vague notion where and how we should meet, and how we should support each other… the whole advance was vexed with cross purposes and with the evidence of a hidden misunderstanding."[97] To Sergeant Pierce, General Smith seemed "lamentably wanting on the necessary requirements for a cavalry officer" and "very unwell" besides.[98]

Waring's brigade went by way of Walker's Mills, three miles east of Holly Springs. There, on February 12, occurred the first of many "foraging" incidents that marked the expedition from start to finish. Lieutenant Cogley of the 7th Indiana recorded that "a member of the 2nd New Jersey regiment was killed at a farm house...the perpetrator of the deed by way of retaliation was shot and the house burned to the ground." More trouble came after Waring's brigade crossed Tippah Creek and reached a point four miles from New Albany. According to Cogley, the owner of the Sloan Plantation "had been a member of the secession convention of Mississippi...when the brigade marched the next morning [February 10] he was a poorer man by many thousand dollars, by cotton and fence rails and meat and meal and corn eaten and taken away."[99]

McCrillis's brigade, meanwhile, crossed Tippah Creek on February 13 and moved to within two miles of New Albany. The next day the brigade crossed the Tallahatchie and went into camp a few miles south of New Albany. Hepburn's brigade joined McCrillis on February 15.[100] Waring joined the command late on February 16. He had taken a large number of prisoners but gave no details, saying only that he sent most of the 19th Pennsylvania back to Memphis with them.[101] Thus far there had been little opposition and no sign of Forrest.

Forrest was in Oxford on February 14, preparing to move east. In a dispatch to Polk, he wrote, "Their troops are moving to my right, crossing Tippah today 10 miles above its mouth on the road to New Albany [and] will move via Pontotoc to Houston or Okolona and thence southward." Forrest estimated Smith's strength at ten to twelve thousand: "Have General Lee's force in position to cooperate with me," he concluded, as if he were department commander. For his part, he wrote later in the day, he would concentrate his forces at West Point.[102] He and the Escort passed through Grenada and reached Starkville on February 18. Captain Elisha Hollis wrote that "we packed horse rations, travelling hard, horses breaking down, and enemy in front."[103]

As Smith's force, now united, moved south, it looked like "probably the most formidable cavalry command which had ever been organized in the western armies." The men carried Colt rifles, repeating carbines and revolvers. The only wheeled transports were the ambulances. Rations not carried by the men were borne by pack animals, along with the ammunition.[104] "The command is in good condition," wrote Grierson to his wife on February 16."[105]

Smith, however, was uneasy and worried. His "morbid anxiety" had not abated. The calendar was unforgiving. Each nightfall underscored his lateness and brought closer the inevitable appearance of Forrest. It was not too soon, therefore, for bitter recriminations. On February 16, he lashed out at Waring: "Your unfortunate delays seriously embarrass our enterprise...

the other two brigades are 5 miles south of New Albany where they have been waiting since day before yesterday, affording the enemy ample time to concentrate or escape just as may best suit his own plans."

Late on February 16, in New Albany, a clearly worried Smith sent Grierson word that Forrest might be as near as Pontotoc. "If this be true we may clinch tomorrow morning…throw out heavy pickets…let your reveille be sounded at 4 o'clock and boots and saddles at 5 a.m…look out for your right flank…do not fight at 'long taw' but close with the enemy…I will hurry up as fast as possible."[106]

Finding no Confederate force at Pontotoc, Smith moved toward Houston, apparently looking for a Confederate force. Then, perhaps remembering the Mobile & Ohio, he sent most of his force back in the direction of Okolona. A small force went on toward Houston. As the road neared the swampland north of Houston, it became a narrow causeway through the Houlka Bottom. The Federals found General Samuel Gholson's men barring the way. Smith reported: "Here we were met by Gholson's rabble of state troops, to the number of about 600, whom we stampeded and drove pell-mell across the swamp." But because the road beyond was still impassable, Smith continued, "I pressed a saucy attack upon the line of the road as if to force it, and swung my main body over to Okolona."[107] As they left Houlka Bottom, some of his men stopped long enough to loot and ransack the Medora house. Details of the action at Houlka are apparently nonexistent. The tone of some very sketchy local accounts suggests that Smith was repulsed and then withdrew.[108] In any event, Smith acted in accordance with Sherman's orders to break off from any inconsequential fighting and follow on with his mission. He would repeat the tactic—a "saucy attack" and then a withdrawal—three days later at West Point.

As Smith approached Okolona and the heart of the Prairie, his men braced for a fight: "Everything indicated the presence of the enemy in force. An engagement was expected at any moment…ambulances were cleared… surgeons placed their knives, bandages and lint."[109] But still no Forrest. A soldier in the 72nd Indiana wrote, "This is truly a rich country. We have been today where no yankee force has ever been before."[110] With no opposition, therefore, the Union force began its work of destruction. Columns of smoke rose first over Redland, an old settlement about ten miles from Pontotoc, "given over to the torch. It was a heap of smoldering ruins. In every direction, except the immediate front, as far as the eye could see, smoke and flames shot up from the burning mills, cotton gins and corn cribs."[111] Sergeant Larson had misgivings: "On leaving Okolona the country seemed to change…Then

General Samuel J. Gholson. A man after Forrest's heart, Gholson first commanded state troops and then became a Confederate brigadier under Forrest. *Photograph taken from* The Photographic History of the Civil War in Ten Volumes, *ed. Francis Trevelyan Miller, vol. 10.*

a change seemed to have come over General Smith…We made long stops on the march, while large detachments were sent out to burn or destroy everything that could be of use to the enemy…Every day fires could be seen in all directions…in fact the expedition seemed all of a sudden to have turned into a raid with no other object than to destroy Confederate property…no haste to move forward or join Sherman."[112] Lieutenant Andes drew a similar picture: "This is a rich country and there was an abundance of cotton and corn…pens on the large plantations then or twenty feet high, joined one to another for one fourth of a mile…barns laden with forage and provisions…destruction reigned supreme everywhere…on every road battalions of troops were set out and scarcely a plantation or a field escaped."[113]

With the Prairie widening out before them, Smith's force began to attract a swelling flood of refugees—runaway slaves. Smith later claimed that because Union handbills brought the fugitives to him, he was obligated to take them in. No other source mentions such documents. (Sherman had no moral commitment to abolition. Whether he attached military value to the destruction of slavery is unclear. Almost certainly he did not send Smith south with any such handbills.[114]) Waring wrote that the slaves left behind them "only fire and absolute destruction…women and children whom the morning had found in peace and plenty…found themselves before nightfall homeless, penniless, and alone, in the midst of a desolate land."[115]

Smith took no comfort in either the emancipation of slaves or in the fires blazing around him. He claimed later that the large number of slaves "encumbered" his mobility, and the fires undermined his confidence in his command. On February 14, he sent word to Grierson: "I am deeply pained to say [the expedition] has been disgraced by incendiarism of the most shocking kind. I have ordered the first man caught in the act to be shot and have offered $500 reward for his detection."[116]

The Union columns moved down the railroad to Egypt, trailing flames and smoke. All the corn and cotton there was burned, and much else besides. According to Cogley, "When the Army left [Egypt] only two dwelling houses stood to mark the spot where Egypt has been."[117]

As Smith moved down the railroad, destroying it as he went, Grierson sought permission to move two regiments east (the 9th Illinois to Cotton Gin Port and the 6th Illinois to Aberdeen). Grierson hoped to cross the Tombigbee at Aberdeen and, at the least, threaten Columbus.[118] Smith assented. The Federals surprised a small Confederate force at Aberdeen, took a few prisoners, killed a commissary officer and seized two ferries, one at Cotton Gin Port and another at Aberdeen. One citizen, Isaac Jarman, died defending his house after firing on Union pickets. They burned his house to the ground.[119] Grierson thought that he could bridge the river in three hours and move on Columbus. The news from Aberdeen did cross the river and reach Columbus, where Grierson's name was enough to cause a panic among some citizens. Most, however, steadfastly began baking bread and biscuits for the Confederate cavalry they were certain would come to their aid. The Mobile & Ohio had already begun dispatching engines and laden cars from West Point and now did the same at Columbus, loading on as much government property as the cars would hold.[120]

But Grierson did not cross the Tombigbee. Nor did he remain long in Aberdeen. A resident commented, "They did not stay here, for they probably had news of Forrest."[121] In fact, Smith was concentrating his brigades at Prairie Station, about five miles from Egypt and west of Aberdeen. The united force would then go on to West Point. During the day on February 18, Waring's men had traded fire with unidentified Confederates near Okolona. On the night of February 19, McCrillis's brigade skirmished again with Gholson's state troops south of Okolona.[122] In his orders to Grierson to come west, Smith not only expressed his earlier fears and remorse but also added a new danger: high water in the streams all around. The Sakatonchee (now spelled Chuquatonchee) Creek to the west, Tibbee Creek to the south and Aberdeen Creek and the Tombigbee to the east—all were high. Sherman had warned him of the danger of being trapped by high water, and he feared the worst.[123] He was not aware, however, of an even greater danger. When Forrest learned that Grierson had gone to Aberdeen, he sent Bell's brigade (now commanded by Colonel Clark R. Barteau) to cover the Tombigbee crossings and the road to Columbus. Barteau moved to the river crossing near the Waverly Plantation, on the Tombigbee between West Point and Columbus. He could have opposed Grierson there if he had crossed. When Grierson turned back to the west, Barteau could then cross to the west bank to threaten the Federals' left (eastern) flank.[124]

On February 20, Grierson moved west to join Smith at Prairie Station. Grierson then led the way in the direction of West Point. Eight miles from there they met Forrest's men for the first time. The Confederates north and east of West Point were from Colonel Jeffrey Forrest's brigade. The colonel, obeying his brother's orders, gave ground and fell back toward West Point. General Forrest did not want to risk Colonel Forrest's command until he had his whole force on hand.[125] There was also the more distant question of General Stephen D. Lee's cavalry force: would Lee reach Forrest to attack Smith with their combined force? Forrest had called for Lee's reinforcements and was under cautionary orders from Lee to await his arrival. In a dispatch dated February 16, Lee had stipulated that if the Federals moved against the railroad, Forrest should only follow them, while he (Lee) moved to join Forrest. Lee had begun that march on February 18.[126] That dispatch was now four days old. Forrest could not have thought that cautionary orders dated February 16 meant much on February 20. Still, he did not want to fight north of West Point—yet—but it was not in his nature to miss an opportunity in a changing situation in his front to damage the invaders. His instinct was not to follow, or shadow, the enemy, but to attack. He also had on hand a more recent dispatch from Polk, much more to his liking than the one from Lee. Polk had written that Smith "ought never to be permitted to escape you or make a junction with Sherman…it is of the highest consequence that this column before you should be crushed…Sherman seems to be lying quietly at Meridian awaiting for the coming of that column…Let him never see it."[127] Polk's words were in perfect accord with Forrest's spirit.

As time passed, Smith grew even more apprehensive. A painful attack of arthritis further undermined him. It is unlikely that his aides had any good way of relieving his pain or bolstering his confidence. Grierson later claimed that Smith was in such a state that he put him (Grierson) briefly in command.[128]

Smith established his headquarters in West Point in mid-afternoon. Jeffrey Forrest's Confederates withdrew to the west, taking up a position covering Ellis Bridge over the Sakatonchee. Some Union forces, probably from Waring's brigade, moved toward the creek, perhaps searching for another bridge upstream. Smith seemed to have no intention of going any farther, however. Nor would he remain where he was for long.

As both the Federals and Confederates neared West Point, some local residents joined Forrest's command. About thirteen men, known as Cox's Volunteers, came in from Siloam Springs, seven miles northwest of West Point, on Sakatonchee Creek.[129]

The Federal stay in West Point was brief, but it made a long-lasting impression on the minds of its people. One resident recorded that "about 4 o'clock the dreaded wretches made their appearance…the Negroes were in fine glee…went downtown to join the Yankees but they were not wanted."[130] Another resident recalled over fifty years later that "we had hidden away many of our valuables. It being the day of the hoop skirt good use was made of its ample folds…our faithful servant Adam remained at hand and never out of call…and there were many others just as loyal to their 'white folks.'"[131] A third resident also writing after fifty years had passed described "consternation everywhere…valuables were hidden away, though I think not wisely, for we children knew where they were…our trusted house boy was mounted upon our best and most beautiful family horse and was sent to notify the plantation agent to run the colored men, horses and mules to a place of safety. The trusted fellow and fine horse were never heard of any more…General Forrest's command passed by our door [the writer lived a few miles west of town]…General Forrest himself stopped to rest under the shade of a spreading oak."[132]

Forrest left Starkville at sunrise on February 20, riding toward West Point with McCulloch's brigade, eight hundred of Richardson's men and Captain John Morton's artillery. His destination was Ellis Bridge, west of West Point, on the Houston Road. The bridge was vital to Forrest. Whether he followed the enemy, as Lee wished, or attacked, he had to hold the bridge. In order to prevent the Federals from crossing at another bridge upstream, during the night of February 20 he destroyed a bridge eight miles farther north and captured about twenty-five Federals attempting to burn a mill at Siloam Springs. Just as important, also on the night of February 20, Colonel Barteau forded the Tombigbee at Waverly. During the following day, he moved his force toward Egypt. If Smith retreated from West Point, Forrest would be at his rear and Barteau on his flank.[133]

Smith, meanwhile, passed an anxious and uncomfortable night. Captain Joseph Karge' visited headquarters and found his commanding officer "propt up with pillows in an armchair, ghastly pale and evidently under great physical suffering."[134]

By first light, Smith had decided to turn back, to escape what he considered to be a trap. He justified his decision later, citing Forrest's great numbers, which he estimated at six or seven thousand men, strongly posted behind creeks on three sides of his command. He could find no ferries to cross the Tombigbee, nor could he ford the river. He thought the terrain was unsuited for cavalry operations. He could not fight his men dismounted because "for this kind of fighting the enemy, armed with Enfield and Austrian rifles, were better prepared than our force, armed mostly with carbines." Beyond that, Smith had lost faith in two-thirds of the men under his command: "There was but one of my brigades that I could rely on with full confidence. The conduct of the other two on the march had been such as to indicate such a lack of discipline as to create in my mind the most serious apprehension as to what would be their conduct in action. Any reverse to my command, situated as it was, would have been fatal." Finally, he lamented, his force had become too "encumbered" by its long tail of fugitive slaves. He could not manage them in the dire straits he faced in West Point. It would take two thousand men out of his ranks. Pressing on was out of the question. He believed he would have lost his entire command.[135] Sergeant Pierce put it thusly: "We had but to return to Memphis with our plunder, which now amounted to 3,000 horses and mules, negroes and about 200 prisoners. We soon found we were destined to have our hands full to even to return to camp. General Smith ordered the retreat early in the morning of the 21st."[136] Colonel Thomas M. Browne, of the 7th Indiana Cavalry Volunteers, saw Smith at the moment of decision: "I waited impatiently the order of march. Just then Gen. Smith rode up in front of our regiment and halted by the roadside surrounded by a knot of Aids and Officers. They seemed engaged in eager conversation. I did not go near enough to hear...but I imagined I saw an anxiety of appearance depicted in the General's face. In a short time afterwards, Hepburn's brigade moved past us on the road we came. Why this retrograde movement?"[137]

Smith planned to cover his retreat with "a push at Forrest" while escaping "just in time" to Okolona.[138] Smith's push is known today as the Battle of Ellis Bridge, or the Battle of West Point. Had Smith destroyed or taken the bridge, he could have put some valuable time and distance between himself and Forrest. But Colonel Forrest had a strong position on the east bank, about four hundred yards beyond the bridge. He was determined to hold the bridge, while General Forrest brought up the rest of his force. Colonel Forrest faced four companies from the 2nd Iowa and 6th Illinois, commanded by Major Datus Coon of the 6th Illinois. With two howitzers in support, Coon dismounted his men and moved forward.

He was optimistic, "thoroughly convinced of two facts; viz., first that the enemy had no artillery at that place, and, second, that the Federal force was at least four to the enemy's one."[139]

Soon after the fighting began, Forrest rode up to the bridge on the west bank, with only Captain H.A. Tyler's company of the 12th Kentucky. Chalmers, who met him near the bridge, described the next moments: "Forrest soon came up to where I was standing on the causeway leading to the bridge, and as it was the first time I had seen him in a fight I watched him closely." Chalmers thought he was "nervous," "impatient" and "imperious." He gave Forrest what information he had about the fighting on the far bank; Forrest's clipped response was, "I will go and see myself." Chalmers thought his chief was guilty of "needless braggadocio" but followed him over the bridge. On the east bank, after about one hundred yards, they encountered a Confederate skulker—a man surely in the wrong place at the wrong time—who tried to slip over the bridge to the safer bank. Forrest saw him at once, dismounted and belabored and berated the man, then pushed him back across the bridge.[140]

By late morning, orders had come to Coon to withdraw. Smith's retreat was underway. It was the turning point of the campaign. The initiative now passed from Smith's uncertain hands to Forrest's iron grip. Waring felt that "no sooner had we turned tail than Forrest saw that his time had come."[141] Forrest wanted to lead the pursuit himself and spurred his horse to the front. Riding toward West Point, as the Federals pulled out of town, headed for Okolona and Pontotoc, Forrest saw enough to know that there was no stopping now. He sent word back to Chalmers: "I think they are badly scared...if they fall backward toward Pontotoc I will follow them as long as I think I can do any good." Tyler's Kentuckians led the pursuit at first, with Forrest pushing hard to get in the lead. Everything was moving fast now. Tyler wrote that his two companies could not catch up with Coon's men until they reached West Point. Beyond West Point, the Federals made two stands, perhaps more. Lieutenant Colonel Mathew Starr of the 6th Illinois wrote that "during the day so many details of companies and battalions were made to assist the 2nd Iowa Cavalry, then covering the retreat, that it is impossible to enumerate them."[142] The first stand was at the Watkins place, about six miles north of West Point. Tyler saw real trouble here: he was without support, facing a rear guard of what looked like 1,500 men, mounted and dismounted, with artillery support. The battery was Lieutenant Colonel Isaac Curtis's Company K, of the 1st Illinois Light Artillery. Curtis's gunners fired forty rounds, trying to cover the retreat. He halted. After a few moments, Forrest came up with the Escort, the rest of Faulkner's command and a section of Morton's battery. McCulloch's brigade was not far behind. Forrest told Tyler to hold his ground while he charged the enemy in flank and rear. The Federals gave way but stood again a few miles farther on, at the Evans' place, at the head of Randle's Lane. The Federals fired a tremendous volley from behind a snake fence and some timber. Tyler came to a sharp halt and was about to order a retreat. Then he heard a familiar voice above the roar of battle. "Close in with your revolvers, Tyler, I am here. It was Old Bedford, charging down the road with saber drawn, full thirty feet ahead of McCulloch's brigade."[143] The Union line broke again. The pressure was simply too great for Union troopers, even with repeating rifles, to hold off the Confederates long enough for their comrades to rally and reform.

R.W. Moseley, whose band had just joined the command, recalled that "we came upon the rear guard of the enemy…we halted to decide upon a course of action…General Forrest with about twenty men of his Escort, came up, but not to halt as we had done, and almost before we could inform him of the close presence of the Yankees, he put his horse at full speed and charged upon them, followed closely by [our] company and Escort, none able to keep up with him."[144]

Pierce faulted General Smith for not sending back reinforcements from the main body to make a real fight of it in the open Prairie where Union numbers might have been decisive. As it was, "the Second Iowa left fifty brave fellows on the field, which was more than we ever before lost on any one field."[145]

Forrest paused only briefly to send out couriers with orders for the next day: to Chalmers to come fast, with all he had; to Colonel Neeley, now commanding Richardson's brigade, to join Gholson near Houston; and to Barteau, to bring his 1,200 men across the Tombigbee at Waverly and move north, keeping on the enemy's flank. He knew by 2:30 p.m. that "Colonel Barteau, with his brigade, is across the Tombigbee and moving parallel with the enemy."[146] Barteau, as aggressive as Forrest, hoped to capture Smith's entire force.[147] He stayed on the retreating enemy's left, camping briefly near the ruins of Egypt. By 3:00 a.m. on February 22, he was less than a mile from Okolona, approaching from the east.[148] Forrest, meanwhile, continued the pursuit until well after dark. Only after coming under fire from some of his own men did he call a halt, about four miles south of Okolona.

On February 21, the day that began at Ellis Bridge and ended near Okolona, Forrest had shown friend and foe alike what manner of man he was. The new men saw what Morton well described: "an offensive fighter

[who] never failed when it was possible to do so, to take the initiative and deliver the first blow…to meet a charge with a counter charge."[149] T.M. Mosely later remembered that "we fought under General Forrest many times afterwards, but this was the only occasion I ever went into battle by his immediate side, and it remains a pleasant memory."[150]

Forrest's men had a second revelation on February 21: the sight of the devastated Prairie. Trooper Hubbard's reaction must have been widely shared: "Up to that date nothing like this had been seen in our part of the country. Our soldiers were angered by the reports brought in…there was a firm-set resolution not only to give the ruthless enemy blow for blow, but to avenge the wrongs done to old men, women and children."[151] Trooper Young wrote that "the men of the command were almost frenzied now because of the burning."[152]

Smith's command passed the night of February 21–22 without rest or comfort. The Second Brigade had halted about two miles south of Okolona, the First a mile south of their camp and the Third a half-mile farther south. It is hard to know Smith's state of mind at this time. In a speech thirty-eight years later, he explained the he "adroitly slipped out of the trap."[153] Certainly, it was not part of his thinking to turn and fight, even on the more favorable ground at Okolona. We do not know if he sensed what daylight would bring. Colonel Browne, of the 7th Indiana Cavalry, however, was under no illusions. The day had been bad enough, full of unrelenting pursuit and mounting pressure, but "we were now hurrying rapidly forward to the day of our trouble."[154]

Chapter 5

"Every Man in That Charge Was a Forrest"

On the morning of February 22, General William Sooy Smith could have thought the worst was over. He had escaped from a dangerous situation at West Point and on the Prairie. Now the terrain ought to favor him. Once clear of Okolona, the road to Pontotoc wound through twenty-five miles of broken, hilly and wooded country. If the Confederates pursued him, Smith's rear guard would have good defensive positions. He should be able to reach Pontotoc and then cross the Tallahatchie at New Albany without much difficulty. It was not exactly a victory, he reasoned, but certainly he had done all that was possible to accomplish his mission. He clung to that interpretation for the rest of his life, notwithstanding what befell his force on February 22.

Forrest saw the day in a different light. It was the last opportunity to destroy Smith on the Prairie before he could reach the Pontotoc Road. Forrest knew that road well; he had traveled it in December on his way to west Tennessee. It would be difficult to bring Smith to bay along that winding road. Forrest planned a slashing attack from three directions on whatever Federals he found in his path at Okolona. Before first light, he sent Colonel Forrest's brigade out to the west of town. Barteau's brigade should already be in position just east of Okolona. With the four hundred or so men remaining with him (McCulloch's brigade was not up yet), he would stay on the enemy's heels as he had the previous day. "Pushing them hard" was how Escort trooper Dyer described it.[155] Although he was outnumbered, he had shaken the enemy's resolve and morale the previous day. They knew how relentless he was. The psychological factors were all in his favor. His great energy was set to unleash a storm of action. "He was an electric storm, a Mississippi Valley hurricane embodied," wrote one Confederate. His confidence spread through the entire command. "We were better riders," one trooper wrote, "more expert with the gun, had been trained to both, almost from infancy and were about as expert mounted as dismounted."[156]

The Battle of Okolona began south of town, where Forrest and his Escort clashed with the Federal rear guard, regiments from the Third (McCrillis's) brigade together with the 4th U.S. Cavalry. Grierson was in de facto command; Smith was farther north either with the Second Brigade in advance of the column or the following First Brigade. As the Confederates pushed the Regulars into the outskirts of town, men on both sides could see smoke rising from fires in town and along the railroad. But what gave Grierson pause was what he saw *beyond* the railroad, out to the east—Barteau's men, drawn up in line of battle. They were not moving forward, but they were an ominous sight. Grierson hurriedly deployed to make a stand against an attack from either of two directions, from the east or the south. For the moment, there was no danger from the west. Two lines of battle now faced each other east of Okolona; Grierson's, about 2,500 men, was longer and heavier than Barteau's line of about 1,200 men. Grierson's right extended toward the west of Okolona, and Barteau's right was facing the northeast corner of Okolona. The Mobile & Ohio Railroad ran between the two lines of battle. Barteau's men were just to the east of the railroad; his line was motionless.[157] Barteau was not going to charge a force twice the size of his unless an opportune moment presented itself. He would wait.

Forrest probably saw Barteau's men at about the same time as Grierson did. Forrest did not hesitate; it may be that he saw signs of Grierson deploying from line to column in order to withdraw and join the retreat up the Pontotoc Road. Again, as at Ellis Bridge the previous day, Forrest sensed that his time had come. He would lead Barteau's men himself in a charge across the Prairie, full tilt, head-on, into Grierson's line. One account makes it seem that he galloped alone on a straight line across the Prairie to reach Barteau. Forrest reported that he made a circuit around the southeast corner of Okolona to reach Grierson. Either way, he outdistanced any of his staff or Escort who may have set out with him. Barteau's men saw him coming. Sergeant Hancock saw Forrest approach and then rein in his charger to "loud cheers and prolonged shouts of mingled joy and defiance in recognition of which Forrest lifted his hat and politely bowed to us as he passed our front from left to right, at a gallop, saying mildly, 'mount your horses.'"[158] When

Forrest reached the right of the line of troopers, he looked once more over the prairie at the long blue line awaiting them. He then gave the brigade its order to charge.

Barteau wrote that Forrest "never seemed to touch the saddle but 'stood up' in his stirrups, an attitude which gave him the appearance of being a foot taller…as he was over six feet in height and of large proportions and necessarily rode a large horse, it was not difficult to recognize his imposing presence."[159] Private Witherspoon wrote: "It was not one Forrest you were contending with, but every man in that charge was a Forrest."[160] The great charge across the Prairie has not yet found its poet or painter. But it is easy even 145 years later to look across from Forrest's—or Grierson's—vantage point and imagine the scene on the morning of February 22, 1865.

Forrest led Colonel Russell's regiment over the railroad to the northeast, driving down on Grierson's line, sword glittering over his head, while Barteau led the 2nd Tennessee through town. Gleefully, citizens cheered them on, waving flags as they thundered by.[161]

The well-armed Federals held at first. When Confederate riders began to fall, Forrest quickly dismounted his men, giving them a better chance of returning fire with their long rifles. Then the U.S. Regulars charged, but they were repulsed. But Grierson could not delay his departure for long. The First and Third Brigades were already moving north. Grierson could not risk being cut off from the main body. He began to deploy some of his units from line to column, preparing to move out. This may be what Forrest meant when he said, "General Grierson left a weak place in his line and I carried my men right through it."[162] It was the breaking point, the moment Forrest had sought, threatening the entire Union command with disaster. Colonel Forrest's men and the Escort were closing in, and McCulloch's vanguard was on the field of battle. Desperately, Grierson and Colonel McCrillis sought help for the wavering Regulars, trying to stem the tide. The 7th Indiana and the 2nd and 3rd Tennessee (U.S.) moved up, but to no avail. It was too much for Grierson's and McCrillis's men to withstand. Panic broke out as regiments dissolved in flight. According to McCrillis, "The Second Tennessee and the Fourth Regulars were forced upon the rear of the column…and the Third Tennessee about to be cut off from the column…all three of the last named regiments became entirely disorganized."[163] The collapse spread with frightening speed. "A stampede ensued. We became mixed up and generally confused…in a run all the way, men falling all around…some from minie balls, others knocked from their horses by the butts of guns, while some were surrendering."[164]

Major William McBath of the 2nd Tennessee reported that "the regiment lost Lieutenant Colonel Cook and 14 men killed and wounded in a few moments."[165] Sergeant McGee, of the 72nd Indiana, saw that one regiment "panic-stricken, broke like stampeded buffalo and ran like wild horses."[166] To Sergeant Pierce, it was "a deplorable scene…the train of contrabands… demoralized soldiers…3,000 lead horses and mules in wagons and ambulances…one stampeded mass, moved like an avalanche."[167] "The officers beat [men] with their swords and cocked their revolvers in their faces to compel them to halt, but failed."[168] The fugitives had "no fight in them…gone like chaff before the wind."[169] The Confederates pressed on, giving them no rest. Barteau, struck by a spent ball and knocked from his horse, staggered to his feet and cried, "Forward, Second Tennessee."[170]

Lieutenant Colonel Curtis had no time to get his guns in position and little hope of bringing them out. Swamped by "fleeing cavalry" on all sides and in the road ahead, he took his guns off the road into the fields. He fared no better, the guns rolling down into ditches and getting stuck there. "Horses and riders tumbled in and the wagons and artillery on top. It was a complete wreck. Most of the horses and many of the men were killed while many were scrambling to get out." Somehow, Curtis got one gun away and spiked the five he left behind.[171]

One brigade wrecked and a battery lost—but the panic subsided and did not overtake the retreating column on the Pontotoc Road. Sergeant Larson gave the credit to Grierson, saying, "To him we owe our salvation."[172] When news of the disaster behind him reached Waring, farther up the Pontotoc Road, he wheeled his command about and deployed most of his regiments on either side of and across the road, allowing the fugitives to pour through the ranks. Waring's deployment was timely, as it now became a different battle. The broad prairie gave way to a narrow corridor of twisting road, giving Smith, according to Forrest, "every advantage in selecting position and to drive and dislodge them."[173]

Grierson adopted the tactics of the previous day's retreat from West Point. In what might be called "leapfrogging," one regiment, or more likely detachments from several commands, would hold a position on the road long enough for the prior rear guard, and other fugitives, to pass through their ranks. The process would then repeat itself. It was tough going for both the hunted and the hunters. Captain Morton credited the Federals' "valiant efforts again and again to take a stand…but each time they were driven back by the determined assault."[174] Captain Hollis said simply, "We fought them hard all day for ten miles."[175]

The Federals' first stand was just south of old Prairie Mount. Waring had formed his regiments "in line with skirmishers far out on each flank... the Third Brigade passed through, portions of it in such confusion as to endanger the morale of my own command."[176] Captain Karge' raised fifty volunteers to man the position—but there was no time. Orders came to fall back again, this time to a much stronger position on high ground east of the road just beyond the cemetery at Prairie Mount.[177]

Here the Federals made the first of two determined stands that day. The terrain was right for a rear guard blocking action. Overlooking the road "was a high ridge, covered with small post oaks and a dense undergrowth, which sloped down steeply into marshy valleys on either hand, that covered both flanks...[where] the Federals rallied and made a stubborn stand."[178]

Waring hurriedly aligned the 2nd New Jersey, the 4th Missouri and the 2nd Illinois along the crest. There was not a second to lose before another storm burst. Karge' wrote, "I had not disposed of half my command when a terrible rush was made from the rear [i.e., south] caused by the rout of the Third Brigade...the enemy was at [their] heels."[179]

Forrest now had two full brigades up, his brother's and McCulloch's. Colonel Forrest's brigade advanced on the right of the road. McCulloch moved forward along the left side of the road. The Confederates fought through the Union skirmish line, but as they moved uphill, the Federals unleashed a tremendous fire on the attackers. Major Coon wrote that "bullets from the five-shooters fell like hail."[180] Both Confederate brigadiers were hit, McCulloch in the hand and Colonel Forrest in the throat. McCulloch's hand was quickly bandaged and he was soon back in action. But Colonel Forrest's wound was fatal. He lived only a few moments, dying in his brother's arms. There are many accounts of Colonel Forrest's death. They all stress how the loss of his brother brought out, with terrible clarity, the general's personality. He gently lowered his brother's head and shoulders to the ground and stayed silent for a few moments. Rising, he quietly ordered his aide, Major J.F. Strange, to see to his brother's body and Lieutenant Colonel W.E. Duckworth to take command of his brother's brigade. Then, according to an eyewitness, "remounting in stern silence, Forrest, taking in the situation in a glance, ordered his staff and Escort to follow, and shouting in a loud passionate voice, 'Gaus [his bugler], sound the charge!', dashed with great fury upon the enemy in front just as they were remounting to retreat and for some moments there was sore havoc in the Federal mass as it flowed rearward, heavily packed in the narrow road."[181] According to another account, Forrest "vaulted

Jeffrey Forrest was the youngest son of William Forrest and Mariam Beck. His father died before his birth, in 1837. His oldest brother, Nathan Bedford, raised him as a son. Colonel Forrest was first buried in Aberdeen, his wife's home. In 1868, he was reinterred in Elmwood Cemetery, Memphis. *Courtesy of the Sons of Confederate Veterans Colonel Jeffrey Forrest Camp #323.*

into the saddle, drew his sabre and then he was a magnificent fury, an avenging Nemesis, such as few men ever see."[182]

While Duckworth led some of his men on foot toward the Federal left and rear, Forrest ordered the rest of the command, now including Barteau's men again, in a frontal assault. He led it himself at the head of his Escort. The Federals quickly abandoned their position and the chase began again.

There was no repetition of the rout at Okolona, however. Historians and archaeologists of the Mississippi Department of Archives and History have concluded that the Federals made three more stands between Prairie Mount and their last and most determined stand. The first was about a mile and a half from Prairie Mount; the second about a half mile farther; and the third about a mile farther on. This short stretch of road witnessed a fast-moving melee, marked by a number of documented events now part of the Forrest legend. Forrest, of course, was in the lead. Major Strange, still with Colonel Forrest's body, urged Forrest's physician, Dr. Cowan, to hurry forward and find Forrest. Cowan wrote, "I had just reached the spot where Jeffrey Forrest was lying dead when Major Strange said to me as I rode up 'Doctor, hurry after the General. I am afraid he will be killed'...in about a mile, as I rounded a short turn in the road I came upon a scene which made my blood run cold."[183] Cowan saw Forrest, with some of his Escort, embroiled in bitter combat with a much larger Union force blocking the road. It was a savage fight, but the odds were against Forrest. As Cowan looked on in dread, Colonel McCulloch and his vanguard came pounding down the road behind the doctor, McCulloch waving an unraveling and bloody bandage as if it was a flag. He "shouted at the top of his voice 'My God, man, will you see them kill your General? I'll go to the rescue if not a man follows me!'" He dashed forward, and men from the 2nd Missouri and Willis's Texas Battalion followed him. The Federals fled, but not before Bedford Forrest, with his own hand, had killed three men.[184]

Forrest lost two horses shot from beneath him. The first died from its fourth wound; the second was killed instantly. The general then mounted the famous King Phillip, a gift to Forrest from Thomas Carleton Billups of Columbus. King Phillip survived the battle and the war.[185] Riding on, Forrest spotted a terrified country woman with several children, crouching on the ground, seeking shelter from the fighting. He sent Cowan to see to her safety.

By late afternoon, Forrest's men were nearly exhausted. Many were low on ammunition. But Forrest knew that he must press on; if he relented, the hunted might turn on the hunters. He was right. According to Forrest, "Ten miles from Pontotoc they made a last and final effort to check pursuit, and from their preparations, numbers, and advantageous position no doubt indulged the hope of success. They had formed three lines across a large field on the left of the road but which a turn in the road made it directly in out front. Their lines were at intervals of several hundred paces and the read and second lines longer than the first. As the advance of my column moved up they opened on us with artillery."[186] Beyond the field was high ground straddling the Pontotoc Road, dominating it from the crest of its prominent ridge.[187]

Unfortunately, it is difficult to determine the exact location of the final Federal stand. Federal reports indicate that the last stand took place at "Ivey's Hill" or "Ivey's Farm." Property owned by Gilbert Ivy in the 1860s, and once known as Ivy's Hill, straddles the main road here, strongly suggesting that this was the site of the engagement. Nevertheless, the rugged terrain does not seem a likely setting for the kind of Federal cavalry charges Forrest described. Recent research into army exhumation records, however, seems to confirm an earlier account by Richey Henderson that the heaviest fighting was farther north, near the "Rutledge place," just beyond Troy. The terrain seems to support the Rutledge location rather than the area around Ivy's Hill or Farm.[188]

Waring wrote that the position was so advantageous to the Federals that "at 5 o'clock, without orders, portions of the First and Second brigades formed in order of battle on open, gently sloping ground, determined to end the pursuit. Until this time Smith had been in advance. By design or by accident he now came on the field." He seemed "brave and cool,"[189] even in the face of a chaotic situation, "the immense train of pack mules and mounted contrabands, which had been corralled into a field near the road, swarmed up with such force as to carry past the line."[190] Forrest recognized the strength of the position but disregarded it. He refused to pull back. If he drew rein or hesitated at all, it was only for an instant. He knew he could rely "upon the bravery and courage of the few men I had up to advance to the attack."[191] He knew that the Federals couldn't fire until the crowd of fugitives passed through their front ranks. Only then, wrote Sergeant McGee, could the Federals begin the "terrible work of our Spencers."[192]

For the first time, the Federals turned on their foes. They charged Forrest before he could charge them. They came down on the Confederates in their three successive lines: "As we moved up the whole force charged down at a gallop," Forrest wrote.[193]

Waring, whose 4th Missouri was in the front line, wrote proudly that the charge showed "all the effect of our three years' discipline on the drill field… 'Steady—gallop—right dress!' accelerated the speed without disturbing the alignment and then at last 'Charge!'…How mad a venture."[194] Forrest called it "the grandest cavalry charge I ever witnessed."[195] His men stood their ground, though the first Confederate volley came at sixty yards' range, leaving "a number of dead and wounded horses and men." The survivors wheeled about, rallied and rode back in with the second charging line, but were thrown back again. They stayed on the field, finding some protection from a fence line and gully between them and the Confederates. Then the third wave came. Hancock described it as "the largest and most menacing" of the three.[196] This time the Federals, many of them dismounted, reached their enemies, breaking into the Confederate line. Many of Forrest's men threw down their rifles, and "drawing their revolvers fought their assailants with the greatest fury at muzzle quarters."[197] Forrest wrote, "About 300 men of the Second Tennessee Cavalry, under Colonel Barteau, and the Seventh Tennessee Cavalry, Colonel Duckworth, received the repeated charges of seven regiments of the enemy in open ground, drove them back time after time…A great deal of the fighting was almost hand to hand…We kept so close to them that the enemy overshot our men."[198]

It was not the Federals' day, however. Very soon, the main part of Forrest's command was on the field. It was not their numbers that told, but the direction of their coming. Sergeant McGee put it succinctly: "The first thing we knew the balls were flying through our ranks in three directions." The Federals fought on, ignoring orders to retreat. McGee said, "'To horse'…

the retreat was as dangerous as the fight if not more so…one tenth of the whole regiment was killed, wounded, or captured."[199] Finally giving way, in Forrest's words, the enemy "fled the field, leaving it strewn with dead and wounded men and horses, and losing another piece of artillery."[200]

The final fight may have gone on for an hour or more. By one account, the fighting lasted for two hours. According to this witness, eighty Federal soldiers were killed on the grounds of the Morrow place or the Rutledge house. The number was probably exaggerated. The dead were later buried in trenches along the sides of the road.[201]

By the time the Federals pulled out, it was close to dark. Forrest now relented, halting any further pursuit by his own men. General Gholson's command—about eight hundred men—arrived at about 8:00 p.m., and Forrest turned over the chase to them. At least some of his Escort went with Gholson, but it was too dark for them to accomplish much. With more truth than he intended, Smith reported that "our march was so rapid that the enemy could not outstrip and intercept us."[202]

Karge's 2nd New Jersey rode ahead to secure the Tallahatchie crossing at New Albany, reaching it before first light on February 23. Gholson's militia men sought to keep up with Smith and took some prisoners at Cherry Creek. There was some fighting—with no details given—at the Tippah River as well.[203] Forrest's Escort rejoined the main command after the pursuit ended at New Albany.

It was a long and tiring march back to Collierville. Few were under any illusions about what had happened. Waring wrote that the men had lost all "heart and spirit." Blame-casting and fault-finding soon erupted. Karge' wrote two weeks later to a friend that he had criticized Smith so openly that the general had placed him in two-day confinement.[204]

In another unpleasant report, Smith is said to have accused the officers and men of the 7th Indiana of cowardice, blaming them for the rout at Okolona.[205] In turn, some troopers openly mocked Smith, ridiculing his attempts to shepherd and herd fugitive slaves and captured animals down the roads. In all, the command that returned to Memphis was completely demoralized, "a worn and weary lot." The retreat had been a "disheartening almost panic stricken flight in the greatest disorder and confusion, through a most difficult country."[206] Horace Greeley commented that Smith "made his way back to Memphis in the best time on record—his van reaching that city at 11:00 p.m. on the 25th."[207]

With the Prairie safe, Forrest moved his headquarters across the Tombigbee to Columbus. There were both supplies and hospital facilities there for him to refit his command. Dyer described the command as greatly fatigued, "our horses in very bad condition."[208] Forrest wrote, "It is sufficient for me to say here that with 2,500 men, the enemy, numbering from 6,000 to 7,000 strong, were driven from West Point to within 10 miles of Pontotoc in two days."[209] Forrest soon congratulated his new, now veteran, command in heartfelt tones: "By your valor and courage you have given safety and security to the homes and firesides of the defenseless and helpless inhabitants of the country."[210]

Chapter 6

NO ORDINARY MAN

Then he said, "Cavalry!" Then he was on his feet. "Forrest!", he said. "Bedford Forrest! Get out of here! Get out of the way!...Forrest! Forrest! Here he comes!"[211]
—*William Faulkner*

General William T. Sherman returned to Vicksburg with the swagger of success. "I got in this morning from Canton," he wrote Army Headquarters in Nashville on February 27, "where I left my army in splendid form and condition...We stampeded all Alabama...lived off the country and made a swath of destruction 50 miles wide across the State of Mississippi, which the present generation will not forget. Meridian, with all its depots, storehouses, arsenal, hospitals, hotels and cantonments no longer exists."[212]

There was no swagger to Smith as he returned to Collierville. He was, however, determined to show that his part of the expedition had been as successful as Sherman's. He cited impressive statistics of destruction: 2,000,000 bushels of corn and 20,000 bales of cotton burned, 30 miles of railroad destroyed, 3,000 horses and mules taken and 1,000 fugitive slaves brought out. He also claimed to have inflicted over 600 casualties on Forrest, at a cost of only 54 killed, 179 wounded and 155 missing. True, he had lost some artillery pieces, but it was the fault of the "imperfect carriages they were mounted upon." Waring noted the loss of over 1,500 horses and all of the force's "heart and spirit."[213] Forrest reported that Union casualties were about 800 in all. There were 104 Union killed and wounded, in addition to six guns, three stands of colors and 102 prisoners in Confederate hands. As is usual in citing casualty figures, conflicting reports make final determinations difficult. Jordan and Pryor, in their *Campaigns of General Nathan Bedford Forrest*, give a higher figure for Smith's losses than Forrest did. The figures in John Wyeth's *That Devil Forrest* seem realistic: "The corrected reports of the losses in the two commands, in the engagements of the 20th, 21st and 22nd, showed 27 killed, 97 wounded and 39 missing in the Confederate army. Smith lost 54 killed, 174 wounded and 155 missing." Most recently, Buck Foster has concluded that "Forrest had lost only half as many men as Smith."[214]

In fact, Smith's assault on the Prairie and the Mobile & Ohio had been intense but brief. Both the region and the railroad showed great powers of recuperation. The Prairie continued to provide supplies for Mobile and the Army of Tennessee. As for the Mobile & Ohio, President Jefferson Davis soon learned that "the trains will run through on regular schedule time tomorrow, evincing to the world the great recuperative power of our country."[215] Trains reached Corinth again in early May. Columbus, the most important manufacturing town of the region, had been spared altogether. Assistant Adjutant General Joseph Brent reported from Columbus on May 1 that conditions there and up and down the railroad were "highly satisfactory."[216] The great want was not corn, but sacks to hold it, and more cars to move it.

As pleased as he was with himself, Sherman found fault with Smith. At the beginning of the campaign, Sherman had considered the possibility of driving on from Meridian toward Selma, Alabama. Whether he could or would have done so, even had Smith joined him, is debatable.[217] But once he returned to Vicksburg, he minced no words: "I am down on Wm. Sooy Smith," he wrote on March 10. "He could have come to me. I know it, and had he, I would have captured Polk's army, but the enemy had too much cavalry for me to attempt it with men afoot."[218]

A month later, he complained again, speaking of Smith's belated departure from Collierville. "General Smith should have moved on time at any and every cost." His orders to Smith had been "as careful as could possibly have been made."[219] The delay was "unpardonable." Smith had had "nothing to deal with except Forrest and the militia."[220]

In a letter to his wife, Sherman castigated his cavalry. Confederate cavalry "with poor and mean horses make 40 and 50 miles a day whereas our fat and costly horses won't average 10. In every march I have ever made our Infantry beats the Cavalry and I am ashamed of them."[221] Regarding Smith's performance, Sherman found only one possible mitigation. In a letter to Salmon Chase on January 5, 1865, Sherman called the Battles of Okolona and Brice's Cross Roads (June 10, 1864, in which Forrest crushed another large Union cavalry force, led by General Samuel Sturgis) "the only real failures in a military sense I have sustained." Both resulted, he said, from Smith and Sturgis "encumbering their columns with refugees (negroes)."[222]

Smith refused to accept a particle of blame. For the rest of his life, he claimed that his expedition had been a success. If he was late, it wasn't his fault. Moreover, he claimed, Sherman had "expressly stated that he could get along without me if I found it impossible to get through."[223] Smith stressed that he had fulfilled, if not exceeded, his orders to lay waste to the Prairie, and that turning back at West Point was the correct decision.

A brief article in the *New York Times* on February 24 echoed Smith's view. He might almost have written it himself. It reported that the expedition had succeeded in spite of Colonel Waring's delay. He had lost men taken prisoner, but they had only themselves to blame—they were captured while straggling, capturing chickens and performing acts not legitimately in their line of duty.[224]

Smith clung to his interpretation of his raid for the rest of his long life. In 1875, he was doubtless glad to see the appearance of Henry Boynton's *Sherman's Historical Raid: The Memoirs in the Light of the Record*. Boynton called the fighting around West Point a Union victory and failed to mention Okolona at all. He credited Smith with surpassing Sherman's performance in Sherman's own campaign.[225]

A less welcome work also appeared in 1875—Sherman's memoirs. By that time, Smith had advanced in his very successful career as a civil engineer. (He was a noted innovator in heavy foundation work and bridge building.) But the year 1864 was not far from his mind, and he rallied to his own defense. He wrote to Sherman, taking him to task for labeling his part of the campaign a failure, and demanding a retraction. Sherman must have found the whole business tiresome but included the letters in later editions of his work. He also included a copy of his orders to Smith from January 27, 1864. In his letters, Smith based his defense—and demand—on two conversations he claimed to have had: one with Sherman before the expedition and another with Forrest after the war. Smith did not date or otherwise substantiate either conversation. In the first, he claimed that Sherman ordered him *not* to set out without Waring's brigade. The claim runs counter to everything in the known record. The alleged second conversation, with Forrest, in which Forrest assured him that he did have six thousand men against him at Okolona, is hard even to imagine and surely did not take place. Smith also brought up, vaguely, the handbills proclaiming emancipation of slavery, distributed across the Prairie. It was these that brought the unmanageable fugitives to him, crippling his mobility and necessitating his retreat. Smith now wanted Sherman to correct his official report and amend his memoirs to show that the expedition had been a "very decided success…We must meet and talk the whole matter over."

Sherman said that he was willing to have the matter arbitrated, an offer that Smith apparently declined. Sherman changed nothing, noting that the official records, when published, would reveal the facts. Smith had hoped for a meeting with Sherman, but the two did not meet. Smith's last word—"Meanwhile I will not let go the hope that I will convince you absolutely for the facts are certainly on my side"—went unanswered.[226]

On the Confederate side, there was but one discordant note. In his report, General Stephen D. Lee hinted that Forrest might better have delayed his attack on Smith and waited for his own forces to join him. Lee was moving toward Forrest on February 17, and Forrest did know of his coming. "Forrest is confident and everything looks cheering," Lee wrote on February 21. "My command will be up tonight."[227] But Lee did not reach Forrest until late on February 22 or 23. He then found "much to my surprise and regret that the enemy had commenced to retreat twenty four hours previously. I had been led to believe, from General Forrest's reports…that the difficulty was in avoiding a general engagement till my arrival." Lee went on: "I am not able to explain his move on the 19th to fight the enemy." Characteristically and wisely, Lee made no more of his disappointment. It was an expression of having perhaps lost an opportunity to do more. He added that he was "confident that this gallant officer acted with judgment and to the best interests of the service."[228]

Lee held Forrest in high esteem, but he had not yet seen the boundless energy that drove Forrest and his men. It was simply not within Forrest's make-up, character or personality to wait for reinforcements in the face of the enemy's hesitation and loss of resolve. He conveyed his own resolve to the men who served under him—even in their first such experience. Few leaders have ever had a greater effect on those around them. Like all great leaders, Forrest inspired men to feats they would have thought beyond them. His men saw that serving with Forrest meant something special: he led them, literally, by example, at the point of greatest danger. They saw him holding his dying brother in his arms; they saw him call an invading host to account for widespread destruction. Sergeant T.M. Moseley, who joined Forrest at West Point, cherished that day. "I consider myself fortunate indeed in being permitted to take part in driving these invaders out of and away from my

home, and especially for the opportunity of riding beside General Forrest."[229]
After Okolona, James Dinkins wrote that "a man who can show that he was
with Forrest the last year and a half of the war is no ordinary man."[230]

Forrest concurred. The men he led at Okolona were "worthy of veterans."[231]
His promotion to the rank of lieutenant general was dated February 25,
1864. Later in the year, after Fort Pillow, Brice's Cross Roads, Tupelo and
Johnsonville, he returned to the Army of Tennessee, now commanded by
Lieutenant General John B. Hood. He led the army's advance into Tennessee
and commanded its rear guard during the terrible retreat from Nashville. He
surrendered the remnant of his command at Gainesville, Alabama, on May
9, 1865. He had made a deep impression on both blue and gray. Grant called
him a "brave and intrepid cavalry general...an officer of great courage and
capacity...neither army could present a more effective officer."[232]

Today, it remains a point of pride for those who claim descent from one
of Forrest's men to say that their forebear "rode with Forrest."

GUIDED TOUR

Okolona has the charm and pace of a small Mississippi town with a rich history. The surrounding prairie remains unspoiled. In town, the streets are lined with antebellum and Victorian structures. Thanks to the Friends of the Battle of Okolona, Inc., a great deal remains to be seen from the Battle of Okolona. The traveling distances are short, and the traffic moves smoothly. A leisurely tour offers great historical rewards.

The tour is in three parts. The first covers downtown Okolona, the second covers Smith's retreat and Forrest's pursuit and the third is an excursion from Okolona to Egypt, West Point, Columbus and back.

The starting point for the first two parts is the Okolona Carnegie Library at 321 West Main Street. Since it opened in 1915, the library has amassed a large collection of sources for local history, including the Battle of Okolona. Mrs. Estelle Ivy, the head librarian, will be happy to show visitors the Heritage Room and to answer questions.

PART I. DOWNTOWN OKOLONA

Leave the library, going east on Main Street (out the front door and to the right), to:

Site 1—THE BANK OF OKOLONA, on the right, at the corner of Main and Silver Streets. The decorative clock was given to the bank in the 1930s by

The Bank of Okolona clock, on the corner of Main Street and Silver Street, is a unique reminder of Okolona's Civil War past. The clock was a gift of the Okolona chapter of the United Daughters of the Confederacy, in honor of Confederate general William Feinster Tucker. *Photograph by Melissa Beck.*

Okolona's General W.F. Tucker Chapter of the United Daughters of the Confederacy, in memory of General Tucker. We will visit General Tucker's grave later in this tour.

Continue on Main Street to:

Site 2—CONFEDERATE MONUMENT and the newly installed historical marker. The monument unveiling took place on April 26, 1905. There was a huge crowd on hand to hear Okolona's Mr. Henry Lacey give the dedication speech. Listeners appreciated his grand classical reference to the women of ancient Carthage, likening them to the women of the war-torn South.[233] The monument's shaft is original, but the stone soldier above toppled into the street in the mid-1940s, according to Mr. Walter Chandler, the eminent local historian. The soldier was heavily restored or replaced and returned to his place, to look out over the Prairie. (Unfortunately, he is armed with

Okolona's Confederate monument at the end of Main Street. *Photograph by Bob Price.*

a bolt-action rifle more suited to a First World War doughboy than to a Confederate soldier.) The marker describes Okolona's importance in the Civil War.

Follow Main Street, and bear left at the monument. You will soon come to:

Site 3—the foot of the OVERHEAD BRIDGE over the railroad tracks. The first Overhead Bridge was built in 1905 over the right of way of the Civil War–era Mobile & Ohio, later the Gulf, Mobile & Ohio, the "Rebel Route." You can look out over the tracks from the bridge. The GM&O passenger station—now gone—lies a few hundred yards to the north. In 1864, the tracks were lined with cribs, granaries and storehouses full of cotton and corn.

For the next stop, go north, parallel to the railroad tracks (away from Main Street) on Fleming Street, until you reach a four-way stop. Turn left on Jefferson Street. At the intersection of Jefferson and School Streets, on the northwest corner (across the street on the right), note:

Site 4—the GILLIAM-CAROUTHERS HOUSE (1896). During the Civil War, a Presbyterian church stood here, and it served as a hospital during the war. There are wartime graves in the backyard. The stained-glass windows in the house are from the church.

Continue along Jefferson Street to its end at Church Street (Route 245). Turn right and proceed until you see:

Site 5—BATTLE OF OKOLONA HISTORICAL MARKER on the left, set back from the road. Just beyond it on the left are two prominent brick gateposts from the old Okolona College, where you can park. You can walk back to the marker. (The college, founded by Dr. William Battle in 1902, was a strong educational resource, particularly in teacher education in northeast Mississippi, until it closed in 1965.) The historical marker describes Forrest leading Barteau's brigade in its great charge on the Union rear guard, drawn up here to protect the Union retreat up the Pontotoc Road, just to the northwest. The marker's interpretation is accurate: the charge struck home just when the Union line began to form into columns to move out. Forrest's pursuit up the Pontotoc Road began here.

The right of way of the old Mobile & Ohio Railroad at Okolona, looking northward. The Mobile & Ohio reached Okolona in 1859. In 1864, the tracks were lined with sheds and cribs holding cotton and corn. *Photograph by Bob Price.*

For the next stop, go back the way you came on Church Street, but turn right, almost immediately, onto a gravel road. The road leads to a small baseball grandstand.

Site 6—At any point along the road you can stop to look out to the right over the fields that saw the first clash of cavalry on February 22, 1864. You are headed in the direction of Forrest's charge; a look ahead gives you the view he had charging across at the head of Colonel Barteau's men; a look back toward Church Street gives you the view that the men of McCrillis's Third Brigade had.

You can turn around at the ballpark. Return to Church Street and turn right. Pass the sign for Okolona High School. On the left, at the top of the rise, turn into the parking lot of the Dollar General store. You can park here and walk across the street to the left for:

Site 7—the ELLIOTT-DONALDSON HOUSE, Beauwood (1850), at 109 Church Street. If you walk across Church Street you can get a better view of the house. Soldiers carried Colonel Jeffrey Forrest's body here on February 22 or 23, 1864, where it remained until funeral arrangements were complete in Aberdeen, the home of his wife. General Forrest was later brought here to recover from a wound he suffered at the Battle of Harrisburg (Tupelo), July 14, 1864. Mrs. Forrest joined him here then. Both returned for a short stay after the war as the guests of Colonel Shepherd, the owner. The house is being restored. Today, Forrest would recognize its external appearance.

Next, leave the Dollar General store and stay on Church Street (heading away from Main Street). Take the first right, onto Washington Street. Turn left from Washington Street onto Martin Luther King Drive (M.L. King). At this intersection, on your right as you turn, stands:

Site 8—the KNOX-FITZGERALD-BRANNIC HOUSE (1850). This house was also a wartime hospital.

Continue on to the *first* entrance of the Odd Fellows Cemetery at M.L. King and Winter Avenue. Turn in here, rather than at the main entrance, and stop at the edge of trees on the right.

Looking out across the prairie between today's Routes 245 and 41. It was here, west of the railroad, that Forrest's great charge struck the Union rear guard, drawn up to protect Smith's retreat up the Pontotoc Road (Route 41). *Photograph by Bob Price.*

Beauwood (1850), where Colonel Forrest's body was brought after his death. General Forrest was brought here later to recover from his wound in July 1864. Probably no other house has such strong connections with Forrest, apart from his birthplace. *Photograph by Bob Price.*

Site 9—ODD FELLOWS CEMETERY. There are two significant Confederate grave sites here, for Colonel James Gordon and General William F. Tucker. Although neither was in the Battle of Okolona, both are important in Okolona's history. After a few steps along the maintenance way, you will see Colonel Gordon's stone on the left and General Tucker's on the right. Colonel Gordon (1853–1912) raised, armed and equipped Mississippi's first Confederate cavalry company at his own expense ($32,000). It became part of the 2nd Mississippi Cavalry. Late in the war, President Davis sent Gordon to England to try to purchase a privateer. Although Gordon could not say after the war that "I rode with Forrest," he could claim another great Mississippi distinction: he had been at Holly Springs with Van Dorn. Gordon also served in the U.S. Senate in 1909–10. Tucker, a North Carolinian who settled in Houston, Mississippi, will always be associated with the Chickasaw Guards and, later, the 41st Mississippi Infantry. During the war, he gained a fearsome reputation as a fighter, particularly at Chickamauga. At the Battle of Resaca, in 1864, he was badly wounded in

The graves of Colonel James Gordon (1833–1912) and General William Feinster Tucker (1827–1881) in the Old Fellows Cemetery. *Photograph by Bob Price.*

his right arm, but he refused to allow the doctor to amputate. He survived the wound, only to be murdered in his own house in Okolona in 1881. The murderer remains unknown.

Continue around the cemetery and turn left onto M.L. King. At the intersection of M.L. King and Wheeler Street, turn left onto Wheeler. Take Wheeler to its intersection with Olive Street.

Site 10—OKOLONA CONFEDERATE HOSPITAL, the largest of the Okolona hospitals, stood at the site of the large wooded lot across the street. There are conflicting accounts of when Federal forces burned it—it could have been in 1862 or in 1864.

Make a U-turn and come back to M.L. King (one block) and then turn left. Next, turn right onto Main Street and then take the first left onto Prairie Street.

Site 11—The LIGGIN-BOATMAN HOUSE (1896 or 1898) is at 104 Prairie Street, the second house on the left after making the turn. There are graves of Union soldiers on the property.

At Monroe Avenue (Route 41), turn right. Then turn left onto Church Street (Route 245 South).

Site 12—The OKOLONA CONFEDERATE CEMETERY is ahead on the left. The best entrance is the gravel road on the far side. The Okolona Confederate Cemetery was established and dedicated by the Okolona Chapter of the United Daughters of the Confederacy as a resting place for "Our Confederate Dead." There are approximately one thousand graves here, known and unknown. There are dead from Mississippi (the largest contingent), Alabama, Arkansas, Florida, Georgia, Kentucky, Louisiana, Missouri, Texas, Tennessee and South Carolina. There are also known dead from unknown states. Cemetery information and visitor registration forms are on hand at the kiosk.

To leave, follow the gravel road behind the cemetery out to the stop sign. Turn right, then take the first left onto Prairie Street, and then turn right onto Main Street to return to the library.

About one thousand Confederate soldiers lie in the Okolona Confederate Cemetery. Both known and unknown, they came from ten known states. Many who lie here were wounded in battles farther north and brought to a hospital here in Okolona in hopes of recovery. *Photograph by Bob Price.*

Part II. Retreat and Pursuit

You should begin this tour by reviewing the information given by the historical marker on Church Street at the site of Forrest's charge (Site 5 in Part I of the tour). You will also need to set your trip odometer at that location. To get to the marker, leave the library and go left. Turn right onto Church Street and return to the Battle of Okolona historical marker you visited at Site 5 above.

This part of the tour follows Smith's retreat and Forrest's pursuit up today's U.S. Route 41. It is a two-lane road and it can be busy. To make locating your stops as easy as possible, set your trip odometer to zero here at the old Okolona College gateposts.

Go back the way you came on Church Street, headed toward Main Street. At 0.8 miles, turn right onto Main Street at the four-way stop sign.

At 1.1 miles, turn right onto McDonnell Street. You are now on Route 41—the Pontotoc Road. You'll stay on this road for the rest of the tour.

At 5.8 miles, note the tall steel fence gate on the right. The view through the gate is of the site of the town of Prairie Mount, which was largely abandoned by the time of the war because of the coming of the railroad to Okolona.

Site 1—At 6.3 miles there is another Battle of Okolona Historical Marker on the right. Pull over just beyond it and park. This is the Prairie Mount site, the scene of the first determined Federal stand on February 22. After reading the marker, you may want to enter the site through the gate. [Note: In summertime, the narrow, unpaved roadway is infested with ticks. Metal detecting is prohibited at all times. The area is watched.] After several hundred yards, the track divides. Bear left. The Prairie Mount Cemetery lies beyond a fence just to the right. You may enter the cemetery. There are two graves of special interest: Confederate Captain J.E. Turner, killed at the Battle of New Hope Church, Georgia, in May 1864; and Littleberry Gilliam, killed in Chickasaw County in October 1864. Gilliam was the founder of Prairie Mount, a former state senator (1843) and probably the largest landowner in the county at the time of the war. According to local tradition, Federal deserters, or "bummers," beat and tortured him to get their hands on his gold, which he had hidden away. He got away from them and hid under the floor of his barn. The bummers set it on fire, burning him alive. With the cemetery on your right, walk just ahead to a small rise. It will give you a view over the field and up another rise where Colonel Jeffrey Forrest was killed.

This page and next: The Prairie Mount Cemetery is all that remains of the old town. Among the graves is that of Captain J.E. Turner, killed at New Hope Church, west of Atlanta, on May 25, 1864. Last is the site of Colonel Jeffrey Forrest's death, just beyond the cemetery at Prairie Mount. The Union line was at the tree line. *Photographs by Bob Price.*

<u>Site 2</u>—At 6.7–6.8 miles, stop at a metal gate on the right. This is the site of the old BRAMLETT HOUSE. Depending on the season, you may be able to make out the ruins of the house. Colonel Forrest's body was carried here en route to Okolona. Directly ahead of you there is a large old oak tree. Local tradition has it that his body lay there.

Continue north on Route 41.

<u>Site 3</u>—At 9.2 miles, on the right but invisible from the road, are the GRAVES of two Union soldiers. They are not easy to find, and they are virtually inaccessible most of the year.

Continue north on Route 41.

<u>Site 4</u>— At 10.7 miles, north of the Natchez Trace overpass, look out on the right for two small brown signs at a small paved pull-over place just as you round the curve. There is more room to pull over just up the road on the right. The signs are for Site 12 and Site 27 of the Pontotoc Historical Tour. At this site are the GRAVES of eleven unknown Union soldiers. To

The graves of eleven unknown Union soldiers killed along the Pontotoc Road. *Photograph by Melissa Beck.*

reach the grave sites, follow the path and ascend the short, steep walk-up. [Note: Ticks are plentiful in the summer.] One of the unknowns may be Sergeant Alexander Brandon of the 4th Tennessee Cavalry, U.S. His friends in the regiment told his family that during the retreat he had been mounted on a mule. The animal bolted, carrying him too close to Rebel pursuers, and he was killed. His friends brought some of his things to his family, and they tried in vain to find his body. It may be that the eleven graves lie beside the original Pontotoc Road. It is theoretically possible, though exceedingly difficult, to follow this trace a mile or more northeast to the site of Ivy's Hill.

Continue north on Route 41.

Site 5—At 11.5 miles, you will see two wooden gateposts on the right, on a rise very near the road. The rise is a slope of Ivy's Hill. You may pull over there and drive up. This is the site of the GILBERT IVY LOG HOUSE (or IVY'S FARM). Ivy's Hill is immediately adjacent to the present highway. The stop here is on the slopes of Ivy's Hill. The log house was at the summit of the hill. The dirt road skirting the log house site is likely the old Pontotoc

This is most likely the old Pontotoc Road from Okolona, looking south, away from the site of the Ivy log house. *Photograph by Melissa Beck.*

Road. Research—both very early and very recent—strongly suggests that the battle may not have ended here, although there may have been some fighting here. Jack Elliott, of the Mississippi Department of Archives and History, has studied the U.S. Army's exhumation records, compiled immediately after the war. They seem to corroborate the account of Richey Henderson (1909–10) that very heavy fighting took place at the Rutledge place, two and a half miles farther up Route 41. The records show that one large group of Union dead was first buried very near Okolona, where the fighting began in the morning, and that another large group was buried northwest of here on the Rutledge place. In 1909, Richey Henderson compiled a "next-to-eye-witness" account of what he called the Battle of Troy. He did not mention Ivy's Hill. In addition, the topography farther north seems much more suited to the kind of cavalry charge that Forrest described as the grandest he saw in the war. [Note: The property owner here insists that you not travel down this road and that you respect his rights as property owner. He is a descendant of Gilbert Ivy, and he lives within a stone's throw of the old log house site.]

If you want to visit the site farther north, drive two and a half miles farther to the intersection of Route 41 and Eddington Road.

PART III. OKOLONA—EGYPT—WEST POINT—COLUMBUS—OKOLONA

This tour allows the visitor to see the wide-open expanse of the Prairie, an old Prairie town, Egypt, the Ellis Bridge monument near West Point, Waverly Plantation on the Tombigbee River and, in Columbus, the Stephen D. Lee House and Friendship Cemetery.

The best VIEW OF THE PRAIRIE is along Alternate Route 45, south from Okolona. Take Route 41 South from Okolona and follow the sign up the ramp for Alternate Route 45. Reset your odometer at the bottom of the ramp.

Alternate Route 45 is a four-lane road. At 7.5–7.6 miles, you will see a sign for Egypt on the right. Take the first left turn to cross the highway. EGYPT is about a mile ahead. Egypt was burned in 1864. There was also a sharp battle here in early 1865, in Grierson's Winter Raid. General Samuel Gholson lost an arm here, defending Egypt.

Egypt, Mississippi, today. "When the Army left [Egypt] only two dwelling houses stood to mark the spot." *Photograph by Melissa Beck.*

Ellis Bridge monument. This monument was donated by Possum Town Reenactors, Inc., to commemorate the Battle of Ellis Bridge, three miles west of West Point on Route 50 West. Although not the site of the fighting, it is a fitting and well-maintained remembrance. *Photograph by Bob Price.*

Return to Alternate Route 45, turn left and continue south. In West Point, there is a sign for Route 50 just before the second stoplight. Turn right at that stoplight and reset your odometer. At 4.0 miles you will come to the ELLIS BRIDGE MONUMENT on the right. There is room to pull off the road, and you can walk up to the monument.

Make a U-turn and head back toward West Point. At the Route 50 intersection (stoplight), reset your odometer again. Keep going straight. At 9.0 miles, you will see a brown sign on the right for WAVERLY PLANTATION (1852). Turn right at the sign. Waverly Plantation will be at mile 10.5, on the left, just prior to the Waverly landing on the Tombigbee. The address is 1852 Waverly Mansion Road (phone 662-494-1399).

The house and gardens are open to the public. There is an admission charge. There is a tradition that Forrest spent a night here, in the Egyptian Room. Certainly Colonel Barteau was here, crossing his brigade over the river just before the Battle of Okolona.

The Waverly mansion (1852), near where Colonel Clark R. Barteau, in temporary command of Bell's Brigade, crossed the Tombigbee River on the night of February 20, 1864, headed for Okolona. *Photograph by Melissa Beck.*

Leave the plantation and go back the way you came. Turn right at the second stop sign (Route 50). Then later turn right onto Route 45 and follow it into Columbus.

To get to the COLUMBUS WELCOME CENTER, follow Route 45 through town and then turn right onto Main Street. The Welcome Center is on the left, at 300 Main Street (662-329-1191). It was the birthplace of Tennessee Williams.

The STEPHEN D. LEE HOUSE (1847) is at 305 Seventh Street North (662-327-8888). Go back down Main Street the way you came and continue until you see Seventh Street North on your left. Turn left onto Seventh Street. It is open to the public only on Fridays, but an appointment can be made at other times: call Carolyn Burns at 662-435-2368 to make an appointment. The Columbus chapter of the United Daughters of the Confederacy maintains a Confederate Museum on the second floor. Of special interest in the house are two portraits. The first, of General Stephen D. Lee, is a copy

Above: The Lee home in Columbus, Mississippi, in December 2008. *Photograph by Elisa Shizak.*

Left: A painting of Forrest by E.F. Andera (?), 1899, in the Lee home. The wintry background suggests December 1863, when Forrest was in west Tennessee recruiting soldiers for his command under General Stephen D. Lee. *Photograph by Elisa Shizak. Permission granted by Mississippi State University to use the photograph.*

of a painting by Nicola Marschall (1829–1917). The full-length portrait of General Nathan Bedford Forrest was painted in 1899 by E.F. Andera (?). The winter setting may be West Tennessee in December 1863. The painting is owned by Mississippi State University.

You may also want to visit the FRIENDSHIP CEMETERY (662-328-2565) in Columbus, where Lee and other Confederate generals are buried along with more than one thousand Confederate soldiers. The cemetery is at the end of Fourth Street South, near the Tombigbee. From Seventh Street North, turn right onto Main Street. Turn left onto Third Street South, right past the Welcome Center (on the left). Turn left onto Seventh Avenue South, then right onto Fourth Street South. The cemetery will be on your right. "Decoration Day" began here on April 25, 1866, with the decoration of both Union and Confederate graves. The Union graves have since been removed. A Confederate nurse, who may have worked at Okolona, is also buried here.

The quickest way to return to Okolona, or Tupelo, is on Route 45 North, through Caledonia and Aberdeen. North of Aberdeen, watch for the Okolona sign and Route 41.

NOTES

EPIGRAPH

1. Harwell, *Kate*, 48.

CHAPTER 1

2. Dinkins, *Personal Recollections*, 132–33.
3. Pierce, *History of the Second Iowa Cavalry*, 81.
4. Crist, *Papers of Jefferson Davis*, 175, 235.
5. Elliott and Wells, *Cotton Gin Port*, 5; also Buttersworth, *Mississippi*, 15.
6. Elliott and Wells, *Cotton Gin Port*, 6–8, 127.
7. Ibid., 2–5; also Busbee, *Mississippi*, 25; Skates, *Mississippi*, 9.
8. Atkinson, "A History of Chickasaw County," 70–71.
9. Ibid., 124; also Rowland, *History of Mississippi*, 35–36.
10. Williams, *On the Map 145 Years*, 18–21.
11. Atkinson, "A History of Chickasaw County"; also Darnell, *History of Okolona*, 8.
12. Black, *Railroads of the Confederacy*, 5, 58, 133; also Cline, *Alabama Railroads*, 51–52; Williams, *Oktibbeha County*, passim; also Henry, "Railroads and the Confederacy," 46–53.
13. U.S. War Department, *War of the Rebellion: A Compilation of the Official Records of the Union and Confederate Armies*, ser. 1, vol. 15, 937 (henceforth cited as *O.R.*).
14. Bergeron, *Confederate Mobile*, 13–14; also Miller, "Mobile & Ohio Railroad," 37–59.
15. *O.R.*, ser. 1, vol. 39, pt. 2, 565–66.
16. Larson, *Sergeant Larson of the 4th Cavalry*, 221.
17. Waring, *Whip and Spur*, 110–12.
18. Pierce, *History of the Second Iowa Cavalry*, 81.
19. Shakespeare, *King Richard III*, 1592.

CHAPTER 2

20. Heinl, *Dictionary of Military and Naval Quotations*, 293.
21. Quigley, *Civil War Spoken Here*, 147–48. According to this expert in pronunciation, Smith's middle name is pronounced "Soo-ee."
22. Brown, "Sol Street," 166.
23. Simpson and Berlin, *Sherman's Civil War*, 588. See also Magness, *Past Times: Stories of Early Memphis*, 110–114, and the note on p. 114 for Elizabeth P. Parr, "History of Collierville" (1949), in a special edition of the *Collierville Herald* (1981).
24. *O.R.*, ser. 1, vol. 24, pt. 3, 574; also Foster, *Sherman's Mississippi Campaign*, 31.
25. *O.R.*, ser. 1, vol. 32, pt. 1, 173.
26. Ibid.
27. *O.R.*, ser. 1, vol. 32, pt. 1, 179.
28. Ibid., 174.
29. Ibid., pt. 2, 61–62.
30. Ibid., 113–15.
31. Ibid., 75.
32. Ibid., 99–101.
33. Ibid., 75–76.
34. Ibid., vol. 31, pt. 3, 445.
35. Simpson and Berlin, *Sherman's Civil War*, 630–31.
36. Sherman, *Memoirs of General William T. Sherman*, 389–90, 394.
37. Ibid., 546.
38. Simpson and Berlin, *Sherman's Civil War*, 584.
39. Ibid., 590.
40. Leckie and Shirley, *Unlikely Warrior*, 109. Leckie cites Grierson, "The Lights and Shadows of Life Including Experiences in the War of the Rebellion," Illinois Historical Library.
41. Howard, *Autobiography of Oliver Otis Howard*, 49.
42. Henry, *"First with the Most" Forrest*, 220.
43. Grabau, *Ninety-Eight Days*, 456–58; also York, *Fiction or Fact*, 136–37.
44. State of Ohio, *Historical Collection*, vol. 2, 519; also Reid, *Ohio in the War*, 884; Randolph, "Memoir by William Smith," 36–39; Sooy Family Genealogy Forum, http://genforum.genealogy.com/sooy/ (August 2009).
45. Welsh, *Medical Histories of Union Generals*, 314.
46. Bearss, *Forrest at Brice's Cross Roads*, 322–23.
47. Waring, *Whip and Spur*, 110–11.
48. Bearss, *Sherman's Forgotten Campaign*, 35.
49. *O.R.*, ser. 1, vol. 32, pt. 1, 171–72.
50. Ibid., pt. 2, 201.
51. Ibid., pt. 1, 174–75.
52. Ibid., 181–82.
53. Ibid., pt. 2, 13.
54. Ibid., 75–76.

55. Ibid., 123–24.
56. Ibid., 251.
57. Ibid., 326–27.
58. Ibid., 363.
59. Ibid., 370.

Chapter 3

60. *O.R.*, ser. 1, vol. 23, pt. 4, 654.
61. Folmar and Williams, *From that Terrible Field*, 145; also Hattaway, *General Stephen D. Lee*, 99.
62. *O.R.*, ser. 1, vol. 30, pt. 3, 197–98.
63. Ibid., pt. 2, 789.
64. Ibid., pt. 4, 576–78; also Rowland, *Military History of Mississippi*, 515–16; *O.R.*, ser. 1, vol. 31, pt. 3, 642; *O.R.*, ser. 1, vol. 31, pt. 3, 743–44.
65. *O.R.*, ser. 1, vol. 31, pt. 3, 641.
66. Woodworth, *Jefferson Davis and His Generals*, 131.
67. Crawford, "Forrest's Race for Rome," 287–89.
68. Johnston, "Forrest's March out of West Tennessee," 143.
69. Robes, "Confederate Generals," 10.
70. Young, *Seventh Tennessee Cavalry*, 77.
71. Dinkins, *Personal Recollections and Experiences*, 126.
72. Henry, *As They Saw Forrest*, 204–5.
73. Wyeth, *That Devil Forrest*, 229.
74. Henry, *As They Saw Forrest*, 271.
75. Hughes, *Liddell's Record*, 150.
76. *O.R.*, ser. 1, vol. 30, pt. 4, 507–9; also *O.R.*, ser. 1, vol. 31, pt. 3, 603–4.
77. Dinkins, *Personal Recollections and Experiences*, 340.
78. *O.R.*, ser. 1, vol. 31, pt. 3, 646.
79. Ibid.; also Lytle, *Bedford Forrest*, 243–44.
80. Chalmers, "General Chalmers' Address," 462–63.
81. Wyeth, *That Devil Forrest*, 251.
82. Berry, *Four Years with Morgan and Forrest*, 262.
83. *O.R.*, ser. 1, vol. 31, pt. 3, 797–99.
84. Chalmers, "General Chalmers' Address," 463.
85. Morton, *Artillery of Nathan Bedford Forrest*, 139.
86. *O.R.*, ser. 1, vol. 32, pt. 1, 346–47.
87. Brown, "Sol Street," 171–72; also Hughes, Moretti and Browne, *Brigadier General Tyree H. Bell*, 100–1; Bradshaw, *Civil War Diary of William R. Dyer*, 35.
88. Chester, "Diary of Captain Elisha T. Hollis," 90.
89. Jordan and Pryor, *Campaigns of Lt. General N.B.*, 382.
90. Ibid., 383; Lytle, *Bedford Forrest*, 257; Morton, *Artillery of Nathan Bedford Forrest*, 143.
91. Bradshaw, *Civil War Diary of William R. Dyer*, 37; also Henry, *"First with the Most" Forrest*, 214–16.

92. Bradshaw, *Civil War Diary of William R. Dyer*, 36.
93. Hattaway, *General Stephen D. Lee*, 108.

CHAPTER 4

94. Howe, ed., *Home Letters of General Sherman*, 283.
95. Gates, *Agriculture in the Civil War*, 38.
96. *O.R.*, ser. 1, vol. 32, pt. 2, 703; also Jordan and Pryor, *Campaigns of Lt. General N.B. Forrest*, 384–88; Henry, *"First with the Most" Forrest*, 219–21; Bradshaw, *Civil War Diary of William R. Dyer*, 37.
97. Waring, *Whip and Spur*, 109.
98. Pierce, *History of the Second Iowa Cavalry*, 84.
99. Cogley, *History of the Seventh Indiana Cavalry Volunteers*, 88–90.
100. *O.R.*, ser. 1, vol. 32, pt. 1, 290–93, 302–6.
101. Ibid., 266.
102. Ibid., 348–49.
103. Chester, "Diary of Captain Elisha T. Hollis," 92.
104. Henry, *"First with the Most" Forrest*, 219. Only one battery appears in Smith's order of battle in the *Official Records*.
105. Leckie and Shirley, *Unlikely Warrior*, 142.
106. *O.R.*, ser. 1, vol. 32, pt. 2, 409–10.
107. Ibid., pt. 1, 252; also Cogley, *History of the Seventh Indiana Cavalry Volunteers*, 89–90.
108. Atkinson, *Dr. John Landrum Atkinson Family*; also King, III, "Civil War Military Activity," 135–36.
109. Cogley, *History of the Seventh Indiana Cavalry Volunteers*, 84.
110. Patrick E. Jones, comp. 1999, 2000, 2002. "Collection of Publications about Okolona."
111. Cogley, *History of the Seventh Indiana Cavalry Volunteers*, 90; also *Story of Redland*.
112. Larson, *Sergeant Larson of the 4th Cavalry*, 221.
113. Andes and McTeer, *Loyal Mountain Troopers*, 74.
114. Murray, "General Sherman, the Negro, and Slavery," 125–30.
115. Waring, *Whip and Spur*, 113.
116. *O.R.*, ser. 1, vol. 32, pt. 2, 431.
117. Cogley, *History of the Seventh Indiana Cavalry Volunteers*, 91.
118. *O.R.*, ser. 1, vol. 32, pt. 2, 252–53.
119. Monroe County Book Committee, *History of Monroe County*, 212; also Evans, "Monroe County, Mississippi Cemetery Records," 184; *O.R.*, ser. 1, vol. 32, pt. 1, 260.
120. *O.R.*, ser. 1, vol. 32, pt. 1, 260, 297; Elliot, *Cotton Gin Port*, 131; Foster, *Sherman's Mississippi Campaign*, 133; Richards, "Columbus, March 1864," 20; *O.R.*, ser. 1, vol. 32, pt. 2, 737. Regarding the ferries, Smith later reported that there were none found at Aberdeen.
121. Monroe County Book Committee, *History of Monroe County*, 212.
122. *O.R.*, ser. 1, vol. 32, pt. 1, 267.

123. Ibid., pt. 2, 451.

124. Jordan and Pryor, *Campaigns of Lt. General N.B. Forrest*, 388.

125. *O.R.*, ser. 1, vol. 32, pt. 2, 753; also *O.R.*, ser. 1, vol. 32, pt. 1, 348–49.

126. Lee, "Sherman's Expedition from Vicksburg to Meridian," 316; also *O.R.*, ser. 1, vol. 32, pt. 2, 753–55, 771.

127. *O.R.*, ser. 1, vol. 32, pt. 2, 779.

128. Foster, *Sherman's Mississippi Campaign*, 131; Leckie and Shirley, *Unlikely Warrior*, 110; also Williams, *On the Map 145 Years*, 46; Hurst, *Nathan Bedford Forrest*, 151; Davison and Foxx, *Nathan Bedford Forrest*, 283.

129. W.A. Moseley Collection, Evans Memorial Library, West Point, Mississippi.

130. Moseley Collection, West Point, Mississippi.

131. Elliot, "Dugan Recollections."

132. M.A. White Letters, Local History Collection, Bryan Public Library, West Point, Mississippi.

133. Lytle, *Bedford Forrest*, 261; also Jordan and Pryor, *Campaigns of Lt. General N.B. Forrest*, 389–92; Bradshaw, *Civil War Diary of William R. Dyer*, 37.

134. Kajencki, *Star on Many a Battlefield*, 126–27.

135. *O.R.*, ser. 1, vol. 32, pt. 1, 257–58.

136. Pierce, *History of the Second Iowa Cavalry*, 85.

137. Cogley, *History of the Seventh Indiana Cavalry Volunteers*, 92–93.

138. *O.R.*, ser. 1, vol. 32, pt. 1, 252.

139. John McBryde, "The Battle of Ellis Bridge," http://www.wpnet.org/Ellis_Bridge/Page1.htm (August 2009), City of West Point, Mississippi; also *O.R.*, ser. 1, vol. 32, pt. 1, 298–301.

140. Henry, *"First with the Most" Forrest*, 225–26; also Chalmers, "General Chalmers' Address," 451–86.

141. Henry, *"First with the Most" Forrest*, 227; also Waring, *Whip and Spur*, 117.

142. *O.R.*, ser. 1, vol. 32, pt. 1, 294.

143. Lytle, *Bedford Forrest*, 264.

144. W.A. Moseley Collection.

145. Pierce, *History of the Second Iowa Cavalry*, 87.

146. *O.R.*, ser. 1, vol. 32, pt. 2, 787–89.

147. Ibid., 787.

148. Lytle, *Bedford Forrest*, 264; also Morton, *Artillery of Nathan Bedford Forrest*, 149–50; Hurst, *Nathan Bedford Forrest*, 150.

149. John W. Morton, in Henry, *As They Saw Forrest*, 272.

150. Moseley, "Cavalry Company of Volunteers," 425, 435.

151. Hubbard, *Notes of a Private*, 91.

152. Young, *Seventh Tennessee Cavalry*, 76–77.

153. An otherwise undated speech by Smith in the Collection of the Friends of the Battle of Okolona.

154. Cogley, *History of the Seventh Indiana Cavalry Volunteers*, 92.

CHAPTER 5

155. Bradshaw, *Civil War Diary of William R. Dyer*, 38.
156. Turner, "Cable's Recollections of General Forrest," 224–28; also Witherspoon, *Reminiscences of a Scout*, 283.
157. Hancock, *Hancock's Diary*, 321; also Wyeth, *That Devil Forrest*, 283; also observations made by Jack Elliott, Mississippi Department of Archives and History.
158. Hancock, *Hancock's Diary*, 322.
159. Wyeth, *That Devil Forrest*, 282–83.
160. Witherspoon, *Reminiscences of a Scout*, 231.
161. Larson, *Sergeant Larson of the 4th Cavalry*, 222.
162. Wyeth, *That Devil Forrest*, 297; also Hills, "And Then I Rode Right Over Him," 13; *O.R.*, ser. 1, vol. 32, pt. 1, 353.
163. *O.R.*, ser. 1, vol. 32, pt. 1, 304.
164. Andes and McTeer, *Loyal Mountain Troopers*, 70. Cook Letter, Friends of the Battle of Okolona Collection. The collection is at the Okolona Carnegie Library in Okolona, Mississippi, and/or the Okolona Area Chamber of Commerce in Okolona, Mississippi.
165. *O.R.*, ser. 1, vol. 32, pt. 1, 312.
166. McGee, *History of the 72nd Indiana Volunteer Infantry*, 272.
167. Pierce, *History of the Second Iowa Cavalry*, 88.
168. Cogley, *History of the Seventh Indiana Cavalry Volunteers*, 95.
169. Larson, *Sergeant Larson of the 4th Cavalry*, 231.
170. Hancock, *Hancock's Diary*, 325.
171. Andes and McTeer, *Loyal Mountain Troopers*, 76–77; also Cogley, *History of the Seventh Indiana Cavalry Volunteers*, 95; *O.R.*, ser. 1, vol. 32, pt. 1, 302.
172. Larson, *Sergeant Larson of the 4th Cavalry*, 144.
173. *O.R.*, ser. 1, vol. 32, pt. 1, 353.
174. Morton, *Artillery of Nathan Bedford Forrest*, 151.
175. Chester, "Diary of Captain Elisha T. Hollis," 92.
176. *O.R.*, ser. 1, vol. 32, pt. 1, 268.
177. Ibid., 283.
178. Hancock, *Hancock's Diary*, 324.
179. *O.R.*, ser. 1, vol. 32, pt. 1, 283.
180. Ibid., 296–301.
181. Hancock, *Hancock's Diary*, 324–25.
182. Richey Henderson, "Battles of Okolona and Prairie Mount," Heritage Room, Okolona Carnegie Library, Okolona, Mississippi, 3.
183. Wyeth, *That Devil Forrest*, 293; also Jordan and Pryor, *Campaigns of Lt. General N.B. Forrest*, 396.
184. Lytle, *Bedford Forrest*, 267; also Wyeth, *That Devil Forrest*, 293.
185. Jordan and Pryor, *Campaigns of Lt. General N.B. Forrest*, 398; Hurst, *Nathan Bedford Forrest*, 154–55; Wyeth, *That Devil Forrest*, 292. Thanks also to Carolyn Burns.
186. *O.R.*, ser. 1, vol. 32, pt. 1, 354.

187. Elliot, "Notes Concerning the Location of Ivy's Hill," 26.
188. Jack D. Elliot Jr., *Findings*, National Archives, Washington, D.C. (September 2005), Records of the Quartermaster General, Burial Registers of Military Post and National Cemeteries, Corinth National Cemetery, vol. 31; also Henderson, "Battle of Troy."
189. Waring, *Battles and Leaders*, 417.
190. Waring, *Whip and Spur*, 268.
191. *O.R.*, ser. 1, vol. 32, pt. 1, 354.
192 McGee, *History of the 72nd Indiana Volunteer Infantry*, 273.
193. *O.R.*, ser. 1, vol. 32, pt. 1, 354.
194. Waring, *Whip and Spur*, 120–21.
195. *O.R.*, ser. 1, vol. 32, pt. 1, 354.
196. Hancock, *Hancock's Diary*, 327–28.
197. Young, *Seventh Tennessee Cavalry*, 50.
198. *O.R.*, ser. 1, vol. 32, pt. 1, 351.
199. McGee, *History of the 72nd Indiana Volunteer Infantry*, 273–74.
200. *O.R.*, ser. 1, vol. 32, pt. 1, 354.
201. Henderson, "Battle of Troy."
202. *O.R.*, ser. 1, vol. 32, pt. 1, 258; also Jordan and Pryor, *Campaigns of Lt. General N.B. Forrest*, 401.
203. Bearss, "Calendar of Events in Mississippi," 106–7.
204. Kajencki, *Star on Many a Battlefield*, 131.
205. Foster, *Sherman's Mississippi Campaign*, 144; also Larson, *Sergeant Larson of the 4th Cavalry*, 232.
206. Waring, *Whip and Spur*, 125; also Waring, "Sooy Smith Expedition," 418.
207. Greeley, *American Conflict*, 616–17.
208. Bradshaw, *Civil War Diary of William R. Dyer*, 38.
209. *O.R.*, ser. 1, vol. 32, pt. 1, 350.
210. Ibid., 354–55, 357.

CHAPTER 6

211. Faulkner, "Shall Not Perish," 113.
212. *O.R.*, ser. 1, vol. 32, pt. 2, 498.
213. Ibid., pt. 1, 257–61; also Waring, *Battles and Leaders*, 416–18.
214. Forrest's complete report, including casualty figures, is in *O.R.*, ser. 1, vol. 32, pt. 1, 251–57; also Jordan and Pryor, *Campaigns of Lt. General N.B. Forrest*, 401; Wyeth, *That Devil Forrest*, 295; Foster, *Sherman's Mississippi Campaign*, 145.
215. Crist, *Papers of Jefferson Davis*, 303.
216. *O.R.*, ser. 1, vol. 32, pt. 2, 565–66.
217. See Castel, "History in Hindsight," 109–27.
218. Howe, *Home Letters of General Sherman*, 285.
219. *O.R.*, ser.1, vol. 32, pt. 1, 260.
220. Ibid., 175.
221. Flood, *Grant and Sherman*, 229.

222. Niven, *Salmon P. Chase Papers*, 6.

223. *O.R.*, ser. 1, vol. 32, pt. 1, 257–58.

224. *New York Times* online archive, February 24, 1864, http://www.nytimes.com/ref/membercenter/nytarchive.html.

225. Boynton, *Sherman's Historical Raid*, 89–95.

226. Sherman, *Memoirs of General William T. Sherman*, 451–57; also Castel, "History in Hindsight," 109–27.

227. *O.R.*, ser. 1, vol. 32, pt. 1, 364.

228. Ibid., 367.

229. Williams, *On the Map 145 Years*, 30; also Moseley, "Cavalry Company of Volunteers," 425, 435.

230. Dinkins, *Personal Recollections and Experiences*, 32.

231. *O.R.*, ser. 1, vol. 32, pt. 1, 351–54.

232. Grant, *Personal Memoirs of U.S. Grant*, 109, 410.

Guided Tour

233. Love, "Monument at Okolona," 393.

Bibliography

Books

Andes, John W., and Will A. McTeer. *Loyal Mountain Troopers: The Second and Third Tennessee Volunteer Cavalry in the Civil War*. Maryville, TN: Charles W. McCannon, 1982.

Atkinson, James R. *Dr. John Landrum Atkinson Family of Chickasaw County, Mississippi*. Starkville, MS: Mississippi Department of Archives and History Collection, Northeast Extension Office, courtesy of Jack Elliott, n.d.

————. "A History of Chickasaw County, Mississippi in the Civil War." Master's thesis, Mississippi State University, 1968.

Bearss, Edwin C. *Forrest at Brice's Cross Roads and in North Mississippi in 1864*. Dayton, OH: Press of the Morningside Bookshop, 1974.

Bearss, Margie R. *Sherman's Forgotten Campaign: The Meridian Expedition*. Baltimore, MD: Gateway Press, 1987.

Bergeron, Arthur W., Jr. *Confederate Mobile*. Jackson: University Press of Mississippi, 1991.

Berry, Thomas F., MD. *Four Years with Morgan and Forrest*. Oklahoma City: Harlow-Ratliffe Co., 1914.

Black, Robert C. *The Railroads of the Confederacy*. Chapel Hill: University of North Carolina Press, 1952.

Boynton, Henry V. *Sherman's Historical Raid: The Memoirs in the Light of the Record*. Cincinnati, OH: Wilstach, Baldwin & Co. 1875.

Bradley, Michael R. *Nathan Bedford Forrest's Escort and Staff*. Gretna, LA: Pelican Publishing Co., 2006.

Bradshaw, Wayne. *The Civil War Diary of William R. Dyer, A Member of Forrest's Escort*. Monteagle, TN: Wayne Bradshaw, 2009.

Briggs, John Ely. *William Peter Hepburn*. Iowa Biographical Series, edited by B.F. Shambaugh. Iowa City: State Historical Society of Iowa. 1919.

Busbee, W.F., Jr. *Mississippi: A History*. Wheeling, IL: Harlan Davidson, 2005.

Buttersworth, John K. *Confederate Mississippi: The People and Policies of a Cotton State in Wartime*. Baton Rouge: Louisiana State University Press, 1943.

———. *Mississippi: A History*. Austin, TX: Stack Company, 1959.

Castel, A. "History in Hindsight: William T. Sherman and Sooy Smith." In *The Ongoing Civil War: New Versions of Old Stories*, edited by Herman Hattaway and E. Rafuse. Columbia: University of Missouri Press, 2004.

Cauthen, S.D. *Mississippi Railroad Heritage*. Madison, MS: China Lamp Publishing, 2006.

Clay County History Book Committee. *History of Clay County, Mississippi*. N.p.: Clay County History Book Committee, Curtis Media Corp., 1988.

Cline, Wayne. *Alabama Railroads*. Tuscaloosa: University of Alabama Press, 1997.

Cogley, T.S. *History of the Seventh Indiana Cavalry Volunteers*. 1878. Reprint, Dayton, OH: Morningside House, Inc., 1991.

Connelly, Thomas J. *Autumn of Glory: The Army of Tennessee 1862–1865*. Baton Rouge: Louisiana State University Press, 1971.

Crist, Lynda L., ed. *The Papers of Jefferson Davis*. Vol. 10, *October 1863–August 1864*. Baton Rouge: Louisiana State University Press, 1999.

Cross, Harold N. *They Sleep beneath the Mockingbird: Mississippi Burial Sites and Biographies of Confederate Generals*. Journal of Confederate History Series 12. Murfreesboro, TN: Southern Heritage Press, 1994.

Cunningham, H.H. *Doctors in Gray: The Confederate Medical Service*. Baton Rouge: Louisiana State University Press, 1958.

Current, Richard N., ed. *Encyclopedia of the Confederacy*. New York: Simon & Schuster, 1993.

Daniel, Larry J. *Days of Glory: The Army of the Cumberland*. Baton Rouge: Louisiana State University Press, 2004.

Darnell, Dorothy. *History of Okolona*. 1961. Reprint, Okolona, MS: Okolona Area Chamber of Commerce, 1980.

Davison, E.W., and Daniel Foxx. *Nathan Bedford Forrest: In Search of the Enigma*. Gretna, LA: Pelican Publishing Co., 2007.

Dennis, Allen. *Mississippi. A Nation of Sovereign States: Secession and War in the Confederacy*. Journal of Confederate History Series 10, edited by Archie P. McDonald. Murfreesboro, TN: Southern Heritage Press, 1994.

Dinkins, James, ed. *1861–1865: Personal Recollections and Experiences in the Confederate Army, by and Old Johnnie*. Cincinnati, OH: Robert Clarke Co., 1897.

Dornbusch, C.E., ed. *Military Bibliography of the Civil War*. Davenport, IA: Press of the Morningside Book Shop, 1987.

Duncan, Thomas D. *Recollections of Thomas D. Duncan, a Confederate Soldier*. Nashville, TN: McQuiddy Printing Co., 1927.

Elliott, Jack D., Jr., and Mary Ann Wells. *Cotton Gin Port: A Forgotten Settlement on the Upper Tombigbee*. Jackson: Mississippi Historical Society, 2003.

Faulkner, William. "Shall Not Perish." *Collected Stories of William Faulkner*. New York: Random House, 1950.

Fisher, Celia Coleman, Robert W. Chandler and others. *A History of Okolona.* Okolona, MS: Okolona Area Chamber of Commerce, 2000.

Fisker, John E. *They Rode with Forrest and Wheeler: A Chronicle of Five Tennessee Brothers' Service in the Confederate Western Cavalry.* Jackson, NC: McFarland & Co. Publishers, 1995.

Flood, Charles B. *Grant and Sherman: The Friendship that Won the Civil War.* New York: Farrar, Straus and Giroux, 2005.

Folmar, John Kent, and James M. Williams. *From that Terrible Field: Civil War Letters of James M. Williams, 21st Alabama Infantry Volunteers.* Tuscaloosa: University of Alabama Press, 1981.

Foster, Buck T. *Sherman's Mississippi Campaign.* Tuscaloosa: University of Alabama Press, 2006.

Gates, Paul W. *Agriculture in the Civil War.* New York: A.A. Knopf, 1965. Also published in the *Mobile Advertiser & Register,* February 3, 1864.

George, Henry. *History of the Third, Seventh, Eighth and Twelfth Kentucky, C.S.A.* Louisville, KY: C.T. Dearing Printing Co., 1911.

Godfrey, Michael L., ed. *Reflections of a Confederate Soldier: Duty, Honor, Courage: Narrative of Obed Mast Christian's Exploits and Diary of the Civil War.* Rockport, TX: All American Historical Publishing, 2006.

Grabau, Warren E. *Ninety-eight Days: A Geographer's View of the Vicksburg Campaign.* Knoxville: University of Tennessee Press, 2000.

Grant, U.S. *Personal Memoirs of U.S. Grant.* 2 vols. New York: Charles Webster & Co., 1885.

Greeley, Horace. *The American Conflict.* Vol. 2. Hartford: O.D. Case & Company, 1866.

Halleck, Judith Lee. *Braxton Bragg and Confederate Defeat.* Tuscaloosa: University of Alabama Press, 1991.

Hancock, R.R. *Hancock's Diary or a History of the Second Tennessee Cavalry.* Nashville, TN: 1878.

Harwell, Richard B., ed. *Kate: The Journal of a Confederate Nurse.* Baton Rouge: Louisiana State University Press, 1969.

Hattaway, Herman. *General Stephen D. Lee.* Jackson: University Press of Mississippi, 1976.

———. "Lee, Stephen D." In *Encyclopedia of the Confederacy,* edited by Richard Current, vol. 2, 920–21. New York: Simon & Schuster, 1993.

Hattaway, Herman, and E.S. Rafuse, eds. *The Ongoing Civil War: New Versions of Old Stories.* Columbia: University of Missouri Press, 2004.

Heinl, R.D., Jr. *Dictionary of Military and Naval Quotations.* Annapolis, MD: United States Naval Institute, 1966.

Heiss, Estelle T.B. "The Life of William Feimster Tucker." Master's thesis, University of Southern Mississippi, 1972.

Henry, Robert Selph. *As They Saw Forrest.* Jackson, TN: McCowat-Mercer Press, Inc., 1956.

———. *"First with the Most" Forrest.* Indianapolis, IN: Bobbs-Merrill Company, 1944.

Howard, Oliver O., Major General. *Autobiography of Oliver Otis Howard*. Vol. 1. New York: Baker & Taylor Co., 1907.

Howe, M.A. DeWolfe, ed. *Home Letters of General Sherman*. New York: Charles Scribner's Sons, 1909.

Howell, Elmo. *Mississippi Back Roads*. Memphis, TN: Langford and Associates, 1998.

Hubbard, John Milton. *Notes of a Private, Company E, Seventh Tennessee Regiment, Forrest's Cavalry Corps, C.S.A.* St. Louis, MO: Nixon-Jones Publishing Company, 1911.

Hughes, Nathaniel Cheairs, Jr., ed. *Liddell's Record: St. John Richardson Liddell*. Baton Rouge: Louisiana State University Press, 1985.

Hughes, Nathaniel Cheairs, Jr., Connie Walton Moretti and James Michael Browne. *Brigadier General Tyree H. Bell, C.S.A.: Forrest's Fighting Lieutenant*. Knoxville: University of Tennessee Press, 2004.

Hurst, Jack. *Nathan Bedford Forrest: A Biography*. New York: A.A. Knopf, 1993.

Jordan, General Thomas, and J.P. Pryor. *The Campaigns of Lt. General N.B. Forrest and of Forrest's Cavalry*. New York: Da Capo Press, 1996.

Kajencki, Col. Francis C. *Star on Many a Battlefield: Brevet Brigadier General Joseph Karge' in the American Civil War*. Rutherford, NJ: Fairleigh Dickinson University Press, n.d.

King, J.A., III. "Civil War Military Activity in Chickasaw County." In *History of Chickasaw County, Mississippi*. N.p.: 1985.

Larson, James. *Sergeant Larson of the 4th Cavalry*. 1933. Reprint, San Antonio, TX: Southern Literary Institute, 1935.

Leckie, William H., and A. Shirley. *Unlikely Warrior: General Benjamin H. Grierson and His Family*. Norman: University of Oklahoma Press, 1986.

Lemly, James H. *The Gulf, Mobile, & Ohio: A Railroad that Had to Expand or Expire*. Homewood, IL: Richard D. Irwin, Inc., 1953.

Lipscomb, W.L. *A History of Columbus during the 19th Century*. Birmingham, AL: Press of Dispatch Printing Co., 1909.

Lytle, Andrew Nelson. *Bedford Forrest and His Critter Company*. Nashville, TN: J.S. Sanders and Co., 1992.

Magness, Perre. *Past Times: Stories of Early Memphis*. Memphis, TN: Parkway Press, 1994.

Mathes, Captain J. Harvey. *General Forrest*. New York: D. Appleton and Co., 1902.

McGee, R.F., Sergeant and Regimental Historian. *History of the 72nd Indiana Volunteer Infantry of the Mounted Lightening Brigade*. Lafayette, IN: S. Vater & Co., 1882.

Miller, Francis Trevelyan. *The Photographic History of the Civil War in Ten Volumes*. Semi-Centennial Memorial Edition. New York: The Review of Reviews Company, 1911.

Monroe County Book Committee. *A History of Monroe County, Mississippi*. Dallas, TX: Curtis Media Corp., 1988.

Moore, Carey M. *Nathan Bedford Forrest and the Civil War in Memphis: A Subject Bibliography of Books and Other References*. W.S. Hoole Special Collections Library, University of Alabama Libraries. Memphis: Memphis Public Library, n.d.

Morton, John W. *The Artillery of Nathan Bedford Forrest's Cavalry*. Marietta, GA: R. Bemis Publishing Co., 1995.

Niven, John, ed. *The Salmon P. Chase Papers.* Vol. 5. Kent, OH: Kent State University Press, n.d.

Okolona Area Chamber of Commerce. *History of Okolona.* Okolona, MS: Okolona Area Chamber of Commerce, 1961, 1980 and 2000.

Parks, Joseph H. *General Leonidas Polk, C.S.A.: The Fighting Bishop.* Baton Rouge: Louisiana State University Press, 1962.

Pierce, Lyman H. *Sgt. Lyman H. Pierce, History of the Second Iowa Cavalry: Containing a Detailed Account of Its Organization, Marches, and the Battles in Which It Has Participated; Also, a Complete Roster of Each Company.* Binghamton, NY: Hawkeye Steam Book and Job Printing Establishment, 1865.

Quigley, R.D. *Civil War Spoken Here: A Dictionary of Mispronounced People, Places, and Things of the 1800s.* Collingswood, NJ: Civil War Historicals, 1993.

Reid, Whitelaw. *Ohio in the War: Her Statesmen, Generals and Soldiers.* Cincinnati, OH: Moore, Wilstack, and Baldwin, 1868.

Richards, Fanny. "Columbus, March 1864." In *War Memoirs: 1861–1865.* Columbus, MS: Stephen D. Lee Chapter, United Daughters of the Confederacy, n.d.

Rietti, J.C. *Military Annals of Mississippi: Military Organizations Which Entered the Service of the Confederate States of America, from the State of Mississippi.* Spartanburg, SC: Reprint Company, 1976.

Roberts, Bobby, and Carl Moneyhon. *Portraits of Conflict: A Photographic History of Mississippi in the Civil War.* Fayetteville: University of Arkansas Press, 1993.

Rowland, Dunbar. *History of Mississippi: The Heart of the South.* Vol. 2. Chicago: S.J. Clarke Publishing Company, 1925.

———. *Military History of Mississippi 1803–1898.* Spartanburg, SC: Reprint Company, 1978.

Royster, Charles. *The Destructive War: William Tecumseh Sherman, Stonewall Jackson, and the Americans.* New York: A.A. Knopf, 1991.

Sherman, William T. *Memoirs of General William T. Sherman.* Vol. 1. 1875. Reprint, New York: D. Appleton and Co., 1876.

———. *Memoirs of General W.T. Sherman.* Vol. 1. New York: Library of America, 1990.

Silver, James W., ed. *Mississippi in the Civil War.* Vols. 1, 2. Baton Rouge: Louisiana State University Press, 1961.

Simpson, B.D., and J.V. Berlin, eds. *Sherman's Civil War: Selected Correspondence of William T. Sherman 1860–1865.* Chapel Hill: University of North Carolina Press, 1999.

Skater, John R. *Mississippi: A Bicentennial History.* New York: W.W. Norton and Co., 1979.

Skates, Ray. "Meridian Campaign." In *Encyclopedia of the Confederacy,* edited by Richard Current, vol. 3, 1032–33. New York: Simon & Schuster, 1993.

State of Ohio. *Historical Collection in Two Volumes: An Encyclopedia of the State: The Ohio Centennial Edition.* Vol. 2. Cincinnati: State of Ohio, 1907.

Steiner, Paul. *Medical-Military Portraits of Union and Confederate Generals.* Philadelphia: Whitmore Publishing Co., 1988.

The Story of Redland: A Historical Sketch of the Town, School, People and Cemetery at Redland, Mississippi. Redland Cemetery Associates, Robin Mather, President, n.p., n.d.

Turner, George E. *Victory Rode the Rails: The Strategic Place of the Railroads in the Civil War*. Lincoln: University of Nebraska Press, 1993.

U.S. War Department. *The War of the Rebellion: A Compilation of the Official Records of the Union and Confederate Armies*. 128 vols. Washington, D.C.: Government Printing Office, 1880–1901.

Vetler, Charles E. *Sherman: Merchant of Terror, Advocate of Peace*. Gretna, LA: Pelican Publishing Co., 1992.

Waring, George B., Jr. "The Sooy Smith Expedition (February 1864)." In *Battles and Leaders of the Civil War*, vol. 4, 416–18. New York: Thomas Yoseloff, Inc., 1956.

———. *Whip and Spur*. Boston: James R. Osgood & Co., 1875.

Warner, Exra J. *Generals in Blue: Lives of the Union Commanders*. Baton Rouge: Louisiana State University Press, 1961.

Welsh, Jack D. *Medical Histories of Union Generals*. Kent, OH: Kent State University Press, 2005.

Williams, Ruth White. *On the Map 145 Years: The History of West Point, Mississippi 1846–1991*. West Point, MS: Curtis Media, Inc., 1996.

Williams, T.P. *Oktibbeha County, Mississippi in the Civil War*. Oktibbeha County, MS: Golden Triangle Civil War Roundtable, 1991.

Wills, Brian Steel. *A Battle from the Start: The Life of Nathan Bedford Forrest*. New York: HarperCollins, 1999.

———. "Chalmers, James Ronald." In *Encyclopedia of the Confederacy*, edited by Richard Current, vol. 1, 275–76. New York: Simon & Schuster, 1993.

———. "Forrest, Nathan Bedford." In *Encyclopedia of the Confederacy*, edited by Richard Current, vol. 2, 606–7. New York: Simon & Schuster, 1993.

———. "Forrest's Raids." In *Encyclopedia of the Confederacy*, edited by Richard Current, vol. 2, 608–9. New York: Simon & Schuster, 1993.

Witherspoon, William. *Reminiscences of a Scout, Spy, and Soldier of Forrest's Cavalry*. Jackson, MS: McCowat Printing Co., 1910.

Woodworth, Steven E. *Jefferson Davis and His Generals: The Failure of Confederate Command in the West*. Lawrence: University of Kansas Press, 1990.

Wyeth, John A. *That Devil Forrest: Life of General Nathan Bedford Forrest*. Dayton: Press of the Morningside Bookshop, 1975. Reprint with foreword by Albert Castel, Baton Rouge: Louisiana State University Press, 1989.

Wynne, Ben. *Mississippi's Civil War: A Narrative History*. Macon, GA: Mercer University Press, 2006.

York, Neil Longley. *Fiction or Fact: The Horse Soldiers and Popular Memory*. Kent, OH: Kent State University Press, 2001.

Young, J.P. *The Seventh Tennessee Cavalry, Confederate: A History*. Nashville, TN: Publishing House of the M.E. Church South, 1890.

JOURNALS

Armistead, W.R., and D.J. Moffett. "Colonel James Gordon." *Confederate Echoes* 1, no. 7 (December 1964): 125–26.

Bearss, Edwin C. "Calendar of Events in Mississippi 1861–1865." *Journal of Mississippi History* 21, no. 2 (April 1959): 83–113.

———. "Grierson's Winter Raid on the Mobile & Ohio Railroad." *Military Affairs* 24, no. 1 (spring 1960): 20–37.

Brown, Andrew. "Sol Street, Confederate Partisan Leader." *Journal of Mississippi History* 21, no. 3 (June 1959): 155–73.

Chalmers, James T. "General Chalmers' Address: Forrest and His Campaigns." *Southern Historical Society Papers* 7, no. 10 (October 1879): 451–86.

Chester, W.W. "The Diary of Captain Elisha T. Hollis." *West Tennessee Historical Society Papers* 39 (December 1985): 83–118.

Crawford, Charles W. "Forrest's Race for Rome." *Georgia Historical Quarterly* 50 (1966): 287–89.

Cuppleman, Josie Frazer. "Importance of the Local Historian of the Civil War." *Papers of the Mississippi Historical Society* 3: 107–8.

Dinkins, James. "Forrest's Wonderful Achievements." *Confederate Veteran* 35 (January 1927): 10–13.

———. "Nathan Bedford Forrest." *Confederate Veteran* 37, no. 9 (n.d.): 339–42.

Elliott, Jack D., Jr. "Forrest at the Battle of Okolona." Part 1. *Tombigbee Country Magazine* 9 (n.d.): 24–28.

———. "Forrest at the Battle of Okolona." Part 2. *Tombigbee Country Magazine* 10 (n.d.): 33–37.

———. "Forrest Wins the Battle of Okolona." *Tombigbee Country Magazine* 11 (n.d.): 30–35.

———. "Jeffrey Forrest." *Tombigbee Country Magazine* 27 (March 2002): 39–42.

———. "Notes Concerning the Location of Ivy's Hill." *Tombigbee Country Magazine* 12 (n.d.): 26–28.

Henry, Robert Selph. "Railroads and the Confederacy." *Railway & Locomotives Historical Society Bulletin* 40 (May 1936): 46–53.

Hills, Parker. "And Then I Rode Right Over Him." *Guard Detail* 4, no. 2 (February–April 1997): 10–16.

Johnston, John. "Forrest's March Out of West Tennessee." *West Tennessee Historical Society's Papers* 12 (1958): 138–44.

Lee, Stephen D. "Sherman's Expedition from Vicksburg to Meridian February 3 to March 6, 1864." *Southern Historical Society Papers* 12 (1904): 310–19.

———. "Sherman's Meridian Expedition and Sooy Smith's Raid to West Point." *Southern Historical Society Papers* 8 (1880):49–62.

———. "The War in Mississippi After the Fall of Vicksburg, July 4, 1863." *Publication of the Mississippi Historical Society* 10 (1900): 47–52.

Love, S.E. "Monument at Okolona, Mississippi." *Confederate Veteran* 15, no. 9 (n.d.): 393.

Maness, Lannie E. "Forrest's New Command and the Failure of William Sooy Smith's Invasion of Mississippi." *West Tennessee Historical Society's Papers* 40 (December 1986): 55–71.

McCain, William D. "Nathan Bedford Forrest: An Evaluation." *Journal of Mississippi History* 24 (October 1962): 203–25.

BIBLIOGRAPHY

Miller, G.L. "The Mobile & Ohio Railroad in Antebellum Times." *American Historical Quarterly* (spring 1945): 37–59.

Moore, John H. "Railroads of Antebellum Mississippi." *Journal of Mississippi History* 41 (February–November 1979): 53–83.

Moseley, T.M. "Cavalry Company of Volunteers." *Confederate Veteran* 34, no. 11 (November 1926): 425, 435.

Murray, Richard. "General Sherman, the Negro, and Slavery: The Story of an Unrecognized Rebel." *The Negro History Bulletin* 22 (1959): 125–30.

Randolph, Isham. "Memoir by William Smith." *Journal of the Western Society of Engineers* 22 (1917): 36–39.

Robes, W.A. "Confederate Generals: The View from Below." *Civil War Times Illustrated* 18, no. 4 (July 1979): 10–13.

Turner, Arlee, ed. "George W. Cable's Recollections of General Forrest." *Journal of Southern History* 31 (1955): 224–28.

Weller, Jac. "The Logistics of Nathan Bedford Forrest." Military Affairs 17, no. 4 (Winter 1953): 161–69.

COLLECTED HOLDINGS

Elliott, Jack, comp. Letter describing Union occupation of Aberdeen. February 24, 1864. Evans Memorial Library, Aberdeen, Mississippi.

———. "Martha Ann Westbrook Dugan's Recollections of the Federal Occupation of West Point, February 20–21, 1864." Bryan Public Library, West Point, Mississippi, 1926.

Evans, W.A. "Monroe County, Mississippi Cemetery Records." Evans Memorial Library, Aberdeen, Mississippi.

Henderson, Richey. "The Battle of Troy: February 22, 1864." From an account given to Henderson by J.A. Whittle, as told to him by his mother, an eyewitness (of the fighting at Ivy's Hill). Heritage Room, Okolona Carnegie Library, Okolona, Mississippi.

———. "Battles of Okolona and Prairie Mount." Heritage Room, Okolona Carnegie Library, Okolona, Mississippi.

Jones, Patrick E., comp. "A Collection of Publications and Manuscripts about Okolona, Mississippi and the Civil War." (Does not include the *Official Records*.) Okolona Carnegie Library, or the Okolona Area Chamber of Commerce, Okolona, Mississippi, 1999, 2000, 2002. Anyone interested in the Battle of Okolona is in debt to Mr. Jones for compiling this archive. It is an indispensible resource, including extensive extracts from published works long out of print and nearly impossible to find. Those who collaborated with him include R.W. Chandler, Greg Cook, Patsy Gregory, Parker Hills and Neal Stehling.

Mathes, J.H. "Battle of West Point." Folder 18, Bryan Public Library, West Point, Mississippi.

———. "Captain Cox's Company Goes into Action." Folder 18, Bryan Public Library, West Point, Mississippi.

BIBLIOGRAPHY

Moseley, T.M. Writings and Collection. Includes "Wars—Civil War—Clay County," typescript probably by Moseley. Also letters to Moseley from Mrs. L.C. Crump, Mrs. Burrows, Mrs. Stacy and Mr. M.A. White. Bryan Public Library, West Point, Mississippi.

Records of the Quartermaster General. Burial Registers of Military Post and National Cemeteries, Corinth National Cemetery, Vol. 31, Entry 627, RG92. National Archives, Washington, D.C., College Park Branch (September 2005), 185–87.

Williams, Ruth White. "Battle of West Point." Bryan Public Library, West Point, Mississippi, 1978–79.

Visit us at
www.historypress.net